"The notion occurs to me that the reason the Japanese are so successful is that they don't have any business schools, or maybe it is because they have all read Mark McCormack's refreshing book. ...it ranks with Townsend's *Up the Organization....*"

—Anthony J. F. O'Reilly,
President and Chief Executive
Officer, H.J. Heinz Company

"I have been associated with Mark McCormack for over twenty years. This book describes the approach I have personally seen him adopt, which has not only contributed to the growth of his business, but mine as well."

—Arnold Palmer

"It's been my experience with super-successful entrepreneurs that they never really tell you how they became successful, much less tell you how you can duplicate their success. Now Mark McCormack has done exactly that in *What They Don't Teach You at Harvard Business School*. McCormack lays out a step-by-step plan on how to be more successful in any business."

—John Mack Carter,
Editor-in-Chief, *Good Housekeeping*,
The Hearst Corporation

"Mark McCormack's straightforward book should be required reading for the executive running a company or desiring to do so. It is clear the author knows how to 'read' people and why he has made such a sizeable impact on the American sports business scene."

—Pete Rozelle, Commissioner,
National Football League

"All that Harvard or any other business school can teach about the functional areas of business is valueless without the knowledge one can glean from Mark McCormack's concise book: how to get things done through people. I wish Harvard had given me a copy of this book along with my MBA diploma."

—J. M. Robinson, President,
Auto Shack, Inc.

"I cannot imagine an MBA course being taught where this book is not required reading."

—Ray Cave, Managing Editor,
Time

What They
Don't Teach
You at
Harvard
Business
School

What They Don't Teach You at Harvard Business School

by Mark H. McCormack

A John Boswell Associates Book

Bantam Books
Toronto • New York • London • Sydney • Auckland

WHAT THEY DON'T TEACH YOU AT HARVARD BUSINESS SCHOOL
A Bantam Book / September 1984

Library of Congress Cataloging in Publication Data

McCormack, Mark H.
  What they don't teach you at Harvard Business School.

  1. Success in business.   2. Management.   I. Title.
HF5386.M474   1984   650.1   84-45172
ISBN 0-553-05061-3

Published simultaneously in the United States and Canada

Bantam Books are published by Bantam Books, Inc. Its trademark,
consisting of the words "Bantam Books" and the portrayal of a
rooster, is Registered in U.S. Patent and Trademark Office and
in other countries. Marca Registrada. Bantam Books, Inc., 666
Fifth Avenue, New York, New York 10103.

PRINTED IN THE UNITED STATES OF AMERICA

DH   0 9 8 7 6 5 4 3 2 1

TO MY MOTHER, Grace Wolfe McCormack, who instilled in me, always with a twinkle in her eye, an awareness that money was indeed worth being concerned about and

TO MY FATHER, Ned Hume McCormack who, more than anyone I have known, demonstrated to me the importance of being highly sensitive to people's feelings no matter how difficult the circumstances.

Contents

Acknowledgments

I would like to thank John Boswell for having the conviction to believe that what I had to say might be useful to others. Without his advice, support, guidance — and very long hours—this book would have never been written.

Thanks are also due to my editors at Bantam Books, Linda Grey and Jeanne Bernkopf, and to Judy Stott, Patty Brown and Jane Williams for coping with the logistics of writing a book from seven points around the globe.

Preface: What They Can't Teach You at Harvard Business School

WHEN I WAS AT Yale Law School I was told that, as a business education, a law degree was every bit as valuable as an M.B.A. Years later, having lectured at Harvard and a number of other business schools, I became convinced that it was—though both have definite limitations when applied to the real world. As an introduction to business, an M.B.A.—or an LL.B.—is a worthwhile endeavor. But as an *education*, as part of an ongoing learning process, it is at best a foundation and at worst a naive form of arrogance.

The best lesson anyone can learn from business school is an awareness of what it can't teach you—all the ins and outs of everyday business life. Those ins and outs are largely a self-learning process, though knowing the experience of someone like myself might make the learning shorter, easier, and a lot less painful.

In the early 1960s I founded a company with less than $500 in capital and thereby gave birth to an industry—the sports management and sports marketing industry. Today that company has grown into the International Management Group (IMG), with offices around the world and several hundred million dollars in annual revenues.

I am probably better known as "the guy who made Arnold Palmer all those millions" than I am by my own name. In truth, Arnold Palmer made Arnold Palmer "all those millions," though I think Arnold would agree that I helped.

While the management of celebrity sports figures will always be very important to us—with Jean-Claude Killy, Jackie Stewart, Bjorn Borg, Herschel Walker, Martina Navratilova, Chris Evert Lloyd, and dozens of others among our list of more than 500 clients—it is only one aspect of what I do personally and what we do as an organization.

Our television division produces hundreds of hours of original network programming throughout the world and sells thousands more for such clients as Wimbledon, the NFL, the U.S. Tennis and Golf associations, the World Ski Federation, the NCAA, and the Royal and Ancient Golf Club. Our marketing consulting division is retained all over the world by more than fifty blue chip corporations. We do the personal financial planning and management for several hundred high-level corporate executives. We own three fashion model agencies, we represent, or have represented, entities as diverse as the Nobel Foundation, the Vatican, and the English Catholic church, and we are television consultants for the Organizing Committees for the 1988 Calgary Winter Olympics and the 1988 Summer Olympics in Seoul, Korea.

In more than twenty years I suspect I have encountered every type of business situation and every type of business personality imaginable. I have had to decipher the complex egos of superstar athletes—and of their spouses, parents, lovers, neighbors, and camp followers. I have dealt with heads of state and heads of corporations, with international bankers and small-town advisors, with bureaucratic governing sports bodies and autocratic empire builders. I have come in contact with every phase and facet of the entertainment, communication, and leisure-time industries. And at one time or another I have done business with practically every nationality on the face of the earth.

What I haven't experienced myself I have observed. Because of our affiliations with major companies throughout the world, I have been in countless executive suites and board rooms where I have witnessed a lot of companies in action—and have realized why a lot of them are incapable of action. I have seen every conceivable corporate style, culture, theory, and philosophy put to work—and noted why a lot of them never do. From my experiences and observations I have drawn the advice in this book covering selling, negotiating, starting, building, and running a business, managing people and personalities, getting ahead, and getting things done.

But in a way this categoric breakdown is misleading because what this book is really about is "street smarts": the ability to make active positive use of your instincts, insights, and perceptions. To use them to get where you want to go, preferably by the shortest route, even if this means jumping some fences or going through a few back alleys.

Can you really learn to apply gut reactions to business? Perhaps not totally, but what you can learn are the results of street-smart thinking. Much of what I say and do in business, from a self-effacing comment to an intentionally provocative one, is designed to give myself a slight psychological edge over others, or to help me get the most out of others. That is what street smarts really is: an applied people sense.

Whether it is a matter of closing a deal or asking for a raise, of motivating a sales force of 5,000 or negotiating one to one, of buying a new company or turning around an old one, business situations almost always come down to people situations. And it is those executives with a finely tuned people sense, and an awareness of how to apply it, who invariably take the edge.

In fairness to the Harvard Business School, what they don't teach you is what they *can't* teach you, which is how to read people and how to use that knowledge to get what you want.

Yet that is exactly what this book *can* teach you: how to read people, how to influence their reading of you, and how to apply or customize both to any likely business situation.

Business situations, of course, are just that—situational. But whenever possible—whenever a definite, conscious act will generate a consistent, subconscious response—I have also done the reading for you. Based on my own experiences and observations I have recommended many specific techniques which can be directly applied with immediate and tangible results.

Much of this advice is unconventional, not just to be different, but because I believe the dependence on conventional wisdom—on old ideas and antiquated methods—is the biggest problem with American business today. Running a company is a constant process of breaking out of systems and challenging conditioned reflexes, of rubbing against the grain. People want to work but policies suffocate them, and it would be impossible to write a responsive book that didn't address this problem and the many disguises it wears.

Business demands innovation. There is a constant need to feel around the fringes, to test the edges, but business schools, out of necessity, are condemned to teach the past. This not only perpetuates conventional thinking; it stifles innovation. I once heard someone say that if Thomas Edison had gone to business school we would all be reading by larger candles.

My main purpose in writing this book is to fill in many of the gaps—the gaps between a business school education and the street knowledge that comes from the day-to-day experience of running a business and managing people.

Over the years we have hired many MBAs from Harvard and elsewhere to work for us. In fact, in my more impressionable days I guess this was one of my own conditioned reflexes: If you have a problem, hire an MBA. As we grew and got to areas in which we had less confidence or expertise, I reasoned that by virtue of their education the MBAs were the best people to run these areas for us.

What I discovered was that a master's in business can sometimes block an ability to master experience. Many of the early MBAs we hired were either congenitally naive or victims of their business training. The result was a kind of real-life learning disability—a failure to read people properly or to size up situations and an uncanny knack for forming the wrong perceptions.

In fairness to some of our employees, we do have a number of MBAs working for us who have made the adjustment to the real world quite nicely. But to assume, as I once did, that advanced degrees or high IQ scores automatically equal "business smarts" has often proved an expensive error in judgment.

A number of years ago the Harvard Business School did a case study on our company for a course entitled "Management of New Enterprise." When I lectured there in conjunction with this course, and later, as I spoke at Stanford, Duke, and other business schools across the country, I began to gain some insight into the nature of the problem. Even in phrasing their questions the students struggled to find the appropriate business school cubbyhole in which to place every conceivable business situation. Then, as if by turning a crank, they expected the appropriate solution to pop out. Obviously neither people nor problems fit molds, and the very act of trying to make them do so distorts perceptions.

There is the old tale of two friends who met on the street after not seeing each other for twenty-five years. One, who had graduated at the top of his classs, was now working as an assistant branch manager of the local bank. The other, who had never overwhelmed anyone with his intellect, owned his own company and was now a millionaire several times over. When his banking friend asked him the secret of his success, he said it was really quite simple. "I have this one product that I buy for two dollars and sell for five dollars," he said. "It's amazing how much money you can make on a 3 percent markup."

I do not have an innate prejudice against intellect, intelligence, or, for that matter, graduate degrees, but they are not substitutes for common sense, people sense, or street smarts. I suspect the Harvard Business School recognizes this as well. I would like nothing more than to see this book become required reading there.

I
People

1 | Reading People

L ET ME TELL YOU two stories. One involves a
future president, the other a high-living golf pro,
and though the incidents happened nearly a decade
apart, they are linked in my mind.

In 1963, I was in Paris for the World Cup golf tournament,
where I happened to have two chance meetings with Rich-
ard Nixon, once at the golf club when he came by my table
to speak to Gary Player, the other, only a few days later, at
the Tour d'Argent, when he stopped to speak to Arnold
Palmer and Jack Nicklaus, with whom I was having dinner.

Nixon's remarks were pleasant enough. What stayed with
me was that on both occasions he used the same words, the
exact same five or six sentences. It was as though he were
talking to stick figures rather than to real people, as though
he had a fund of stock phrases for every type of person he
was likely to meet—five or six sentences for a sports
personality, a paragraph for a business leader, another for a
religious figure.

The other incident involved the flamboyant golfer Doug
Sanders. When we first started representing Doug a lot of
people told me we had made a mistake. Doug did have
some "Vegas" in him. He ran with a fast crowd, got into his
share of scrapes, and was known to make more than just a
friendly wager every now and then. Some people thought

he was too controversial for us and asked why I trusted him. Quite frankly, I trusted Doug Sanders a lot more than some of the people who were questioning me. Which brings me to my story.

Once Doug played a golf exhibition up in Canada. He made all the arrangements himself. I didn't know anything about it, and since apparently he was paid in cash I probably never would have known anything about it. But about a week after the exhibition took place, we received an envelope from Doug. There was no letter or note inside, only our commission—in cash.

I recall these incidents now because they demonstrate something important about reading people. What people say and do in the most innocent situations can speak volumes about their real selves.

My accidental encounters with Nixon, for instance, indicated a certain insincerity and a degree of phoniness that I remembered ten years later, when he was forced to resign the presidency. Nixon's troubles probably had as much to do with his phoniness as they did with Watergate. People don't like phonies. They don't trust them, and they certainly don't want one running their country.

In Doug Sanders's case, the fee for the exhibition was so insignificant it might not have seemed worth the bother. But to this day I can see Doug going back to his hotel room, pulling a wad of cash out of his pocket, counting out our commission, sticking it in an envelope, and scribbling out our address. This was so totally in keeping with Doug Sanders's character that nothing else would have occurred to him.

One would like to believe that it was a future American president who exhibited quality of character and a golf hustler who came off as a con man. But the facts in these cases belie those conclusions.

What does this have to do with business? Everything.

In the business world it is easy enough to adopt a corporate persona, or several corporate personae, depending on the situation. Some people will act one way with their subordinates, another way with their boss, and a totally different way with people outside their company.

But the real self—one's true nature—can't change color to suit its environment. In any ongoing business situation, sooner or later—either subliminally or out in the open—you are going to find that you are dealing with that person's real self.

If nothing else, you want to hear what people are really saying, as opposed to what they are telling you; you want to be able to put someone's deeds—his own business activities—into the larger context of character. Whether I'm selling or buying, whether I'm hiring or (in our capacity as consultants) being hired; whether I'm negotiating a contract or responding to someone else's demands, I want to know where the other person is coming from. I want to know the other person's real self.

Business situations always come down to people situations. And the more—and the sooner—I know about the person I am dealing with, the more effective I'm going to be.

Don't Take Notions for an Answer

People will often make judgments about others even before meeting them based on what they've heard or what they know about their company. They will even mistrust or ignore their own perceptions so as to make them conform to foregone conclusions.

At IMG we often have to face the preconceived notions that exist about our own company. What we do is fairly visible, and a number of the magazine and television profiles about IMG or me have stressed our power position in sports and painted us as tough, even ruthless negotiators.

Nine out of ten times this works to our advantage. People

expect us to name big numbers, and their anticipation often makes it easier for us to get them. And when they find that we are actually fairly reasonable people to deal with, they are bowled over.

But there is also every tenth guy who has so hardened himself to his preconceived notions that he has no perception of the business situation itself or of the people from our company with whom he is dealing. He is so prepared to be tough himself, or to defend against our toughness, that he takes "Nice to meet you" as a veiled threat. Obviously his preconceived notions have made him incapable of any genuinely revealing insights.

People reading is a matter of opening up your senses to what is really going on and converting this insight into tangible evidence that can be used to your advantage.

Dave DeBusschere, the former basketball star, was a vice-president of our television company for several years prior to his assuming his present position as general manager of the New York Knicks. Dave once had several frustrating meetings with an executive of an insurance company in Connecticut whom he was trying to interest in sponsoring one of our television shows. The executive seemed genuinely interested in the concept but was so overwhelmed to be dealing with Dave DeBusschere he could never get past this fact, or his own suspicions. If this was such a great opportunity, he reasoned, then how come just a "regular guy" wasn't trying to sell it to him?

Use Your Insight

Dave Marr, the former PGA golf champion, and I were once joking about some of the great golf hustlers we had known when Dave came up with the First Axiom of Golf Wagering: "Never bet with anyone you meet on the first tee," he said, "who has a deep suntan, a one-iron in his bag, and squinty eyes."

Shrewd insights into people can be gained simply through the powers of observation. In most business situations there is usually more to see than meets the eye, a whole level of personal dynamics operating just beneath the surface.

Most business situations provide all sorts of tangible evidence that allows you to see beneath the surface. Sometimes these are the things that people say and do unconsciously, the way someone looks away at the sound of a particular question, for instance. But they may also be acts that are neither simple nor unconscious, such as the way someone chooses to phrase a particular thought. The point is that the clues for insight abound and are there to be used by anyone who is tuned in to them.

A surprising number of executives are not. They totally lack an awareness of what is really going on around them. Either they are too busy listening to themselves to listen to anyone else or too involved in their own corporate presence to notice what someone else might be doing.

I can't imagine anyone being effective in business without having some insight into people. Business itself is such a subtle matter of taking a slight edge here, an imperceptible edge there. And every aspect of the process comes back to people—managing them, selling to them, working with them, simply getting them to do what you want them to do. Without insight there is no subtlety.

Insight allows you to see beyond the present. Suppose you had a way of knowing everything that was going to happen in business over the next ten years. That information would not only make you wise; it would also make you successful and wealthy. Yet it is your insight into people that gives you the ability to predict the future.

A person's true nature, true self, cannot change with situations. It is totally consistent. The better you know that person, the more you can get beneath the facades, the more accurately you can predict how he or she is likely to react or respond in almost any business situation. This knowledge can be invaluable.

The process of course is precisely the *modus operandi* of the "professionals"—the psychics and fortune tellers, who have been using the same tricks to tell the future for centuries.

Psychics will size up their clients by observing them— how they act, how they look, what they're wearing—and by asking a few innocent questions. From this information they can "see into the future," which is really a matter of telling their client what he or she wants to hear based on what has already been found out. The good ones can come up with some startlingly perceptive things based on the tiniest pieces of information. There are probably some psychics who would make excellent business executives.

I also know a lot of business executives who would make terrible psychics.

Insight demands opening up your senses, talking less and listening more. I believe you can learn almost everything you need to know—and more than other people would like you to know—simply by watching and listening, keeping your eyes peeled, your ears open. And your mouth closed.

Listen Aggressively

The ability to listen, really to hear what someone is saying, has far greater business implications, of course, than simply gaining insight into people. In selling, for instance, there is probably no greater asset. But the bottom line is that almost any business situation will be handled differently, and with different results, by someone who is listening and someone who isn't.

When I was preparing to write this book I asked a number of my business friends, several of them chairmen of companies, what business advice they would give if they were writing it. Almost without exception, and often at the top of their lists, they said, "Learn to be a good listener."

One friend, the head of a well-known sales organization, described it as "Watch your listen/talk ratio." Another, an executive at Pepsi Cola, told me the story of one of Pepsi's all-time corporate coups and how if he had been a better listener he would have saved himself and his company a lot of time.

Pepsi, he said, had been trying forever to get into Burger King, and since they believed Burger King would never dream of dropping Coke, the focus of their presentation was always toward giving the consumer a choice. Burger King's philosophy did indeed promote choice ("Have it your way"), but, as Pepsi was told time and again, this was in the larger, quality control philosophy of a limited menu, *including one cola*.

One day, Pepsi finally got the hint and changed its pitch to stress that Pepsi and Burger King were corporate soul mates—the number twos going after the number ones. Since they already shared mutual strategies of "product superiority" (the Pepsi Challenge; Broiling Beats Frying), wouldn't it make sense to kick out Coke and bring in Pepsi?

"You know," someone at Burger King said, "we've been trying to tell you that for months. I'm glad someone finally listened."

Observe Aggressively

I will often fly great distances to meet someone face to face, even when I can say much of what needs to be said over the phone. If it's important, or if it's a relationship that may be long term, I want to form impressions based on what I observe even more than on what I hear. After all, the impression you have from meeting someone in person is often quite different from that formed in speaking over the phone.

Observation is an aggressive act. People are constantly revealing themselves in ways that will go unnoticed unless you are aggressively involved in noticing them.

The statements people make about themselves, the signals they give off, are both conscious and unconscious. "Body language," as these unconscious signals are commonly called, is certainly important, but it isn't even half the story. Most visual statements are quite conscious and intentional—the way someone dresses, the way he carries himself, and all the other ways people go about trying to create a particular impression. But these signals are only as useful as your ability to pick them up.

Aggressive observation means going after the big picture, taking all these conscious and unconscious signals, weighing them, and converting them into usable perceptions. When I meet someone face to face, what I am trying to establish more than anything else is a comfort zone—the "picture frame," so to speak—or the boundaries I need to observe, based on what I see and hear, which will best enable me to deal with that person.

Aggressive observation does not mean hasty observation—jumping too quickly to conclusions, overresponding to conventional interpretations, or reading meaning into things where none exists. For instance, when I am meeting at someone else's office, I have often noticed that people will sort of "lean in" to the situation when they are ready to get serious, even unconsciously using their hands to push everything on their desk a couple of inches forward. Yet almost as often I have seen people at this same point lean back in their chairs and feign a totally relaxed position.

To generalize about either, then, or to jump to some hasty conclusion, would be as foolish as it would be misleading. Almost any useful observation must be considered within the larger context of the situation and what else you are hearing and seeing.

Conventional wisdom says that if someone slumps in the

chair he or she is not very "commanding"; the converse also supposedly holds true. But how many of us have, at one time or another, dealt with the "glad hander," the guy who sits erect on the edge of his chair, leans slightly forward, hangs on your every word—and then never does anything. These are often the old school "I'm-glad-you-asked-me-that" types, or the too-eager beavers, the young fast-trackers who have already decided that it is not what they do and say but how they look along the way that is going to get them to the top. People who are a little too erect, a little too attentive, make me nervous.

Posture is also interesting for another reason. One of the most useful observations you can make about people is the relative importance they place on form in relation to substance. There's a world of difference between posture and postur*ing*.

It bothers me when people strike a pose, when their casualness is a little too studied, or their efforts to bulk up their physique or suck in their stomach are a little too strained. The offices of these people, or how they choose to decorate them, are often an extension of this. An office that is overly cluttered with diplomas and mementos or is obviously contrived to create a certain impression is usually a dead giveaway. You have to be careful in dealing with people of this sort. They are more likely to be interested in looks than in performance, in appearances rather than real accomplishment.

Of course, the most fertile, consistent, revealing arena for observation is the eyes. The eyes will tell you more than anything else what someone is really thinking, even when all the other signs are pointing elsewhere.

Remember that people communicate with their eyes in business situations when they can't use words. The next time you're in a meeting with more than one person from outside your company, notice their eye contact with each other. It will help you determine what they are really thinking, reveal who among them is most influential—and let you know whether you are boring them to tears.

Ergo Ego

Ego makes the difference—the difference between theory and practice, between wishful thinking and real life, between the way things work and the way you would like them to work, between what they can teach you at Harvard Business School and what they can't. In a company of 2,500 people there are 2,500 egos running around, each with his or her unique view of reality. Ego is why some things that should happen don't, why other things that shouldn't happen do, and why both take a lot longer than necessary.

A person's ego, even an overbearing one, may be your strongest ally. A lot of deals get made simply because someone's ego is so involved that psychologically he can't afford *not* to get it done. If you can read ego, understand its impact on business events, then control it by either stroking it, poking at it, or minimizing its damage, you can be the beneficiary of many of these deals.

The size of someone's ego is by far the easiest thing to figure out about him. Most successful businessmen are one giant ego with a couple of arms and legs sticking out. (Interestingly, and as a generalization, most women in business are somewhat harder to read. Even today a woman's sense of self—how she defines herself—is less wrapped up in her job than is that of her male counterparts.)

But a giant ego doesn't mean a strong ego. In fact, it often means the opposite, that someone feels the need to be assertive because of a low self-image. And a small ego doesn't necessarily indicate weakness. Many of the most effective people I know in business are very low-key.

I prefer to deal with strong egos, as I'm sure most people in business do. These are usually the executives who are willing to take reasonable risks, don't second-guess, and are the quickest to get things done.

Weaker egos are harder to read, which makes it more difficult to determine your own course of action. They also operate with lower expectations of themselves—which means that dealing with them will take more time and you will accomplish less.

Once you have determined the strength of a person's ego, you can cope with a range of pragmatic questions: How direct and forthright are his answers? How quickly will he make a decision, and once he has made it will he vacillate? Is he consistent? Is he up-front or would he rather operate from behind a wall? Does he deal with the facts as they are or as he would like them to be?

And, most important of all: How secure is this person?

A person's "security quotient" has a direct bearing on how he will behave in business situations. Will he be stubborn or reasonable? Will form be more important than substance? What excesses and vanities will probably come into play? Is he likely to say one thing and do another? Does he prefer to deal to your face . . . or to your back?

Instead of always challenging or confronting the other person's ego, it is much easier and far more effective to acknowledge and understand its impact on your business and use this information to your advantage.

One final question of ego needs to be considered, and that is your own. Nothing blocks insight into other people more than your own ego. Be aware of your strengths and weaknesses and how these are likely to slant your reaction to others. It is difficult to be effective if your conclusions about what makes someone tick are based on your ego rather than on his.

Useful Impressions

On any number of occasions I have gone into situations which ultimately did not work out the way I would have liked and yet my favorable impression of the other party— how he or she handled the situation—made me want to deal with that person again. This has often led to opportunities that did work—and that more than compensated for any initial disappointments.

When we first tried to represent Chris Evert in 1975, she decided to remain independent. But in the course of our series of meetings, I was so impressed with her character, her directness, and the way she handled herself that I was convinced that there was a "rightness" to the relationship and determined that one day we would represent her. Five years later she became a client.

I have also come out of other situations and thought, "Boy, am I glad that's over." And while I have never unilaterally decided that I would not deal with someone again under any circumstances, with some people those circumstances would have to be very special. When I was young I was more impressed by outward factors—money, power, and glamour. But as I grow older and, theoretically, wiser, I've come to appreciate the importance of business character and other inner qualities and to see the relative insignificance of outward glitter, be it celebrity, position, or appearances.

People who are impressed by the superficial should make you wonder how easy it would be to pull the wool over their eyes in a business dealing.

Be alert to the business acquaintance who refers to his very "close friend" (usually someone whose name is calculated to impress) or implies that he has a strong personal relationship with a particular associate. If you happen to know the person being claimed as a friend, you might want to get that person's version of the relationship. If it turns out that they have met only once or twice, you might start thinking more about the accuracy of his other statements. (I once called an employee on this—a man I knew had *never* met the person he was referring to as his "best friend." He gave me one of the best comebacks I have ever heard. "What I meant," he said, "is that he is one my best *phone* friends.")

The people who work with someone can provide revealing information about that person. A secretary who makes a strong impression, for instance, may help you form a perception of his or her boss.

The same thing goes for other subordinates. I had a series of meetings with a high-ranking executive at a well-known sporting goods company. He had a reputation as fairly competent, but he seemed totally cowed and reluctant to commit to even the most mundane details. When I met with his boss, the company's chairman, I was prepared for what I found—a man whose ego demanded that he make all the decisions.

People within a corporation tend to pick up many of the characteristics of their superiors. If you know their boss, you can learn quite a bit by judging how well they have adopted their boss's strengths and assets as opposed to his weaknesses or more questionable practices.

Several years ago I was having lunch in Australia with the director of one of the major television stations there. He was a well-known figure in his own right, but his boss, the owner of an international communications conglomerate, was one of the most powerful and recognizable men in all of Australia.

I had lunched with the director's boss on a score of occasions and knew that he never signed a restaurant check. At the end of the meal he simply got up and left. It was probably a vanity, albeit an impressive one: Either he had an account with every restaurant in Australia or his habit was so well known that any restaurant he patronized knew to bill his office.

In any event, the day of our lunch the station director adopted this particular habit of his superior. As I was about to ask for the check, the director announced it had already been taken care of. Then, with some flourish, he got up from the table and walked out of the restaurant. The only problem was that he was not nearly as well known as his boss. Much to his embarrassment, an anxious maitre d', who thought the man was trying to jump the check, chased him down the street.

Obviously there are no hard and fast rules for reading people or gaining insight into the personalities beneath their corporate disguises. But if a point of reference exists, if there is some basis for comparison, either to a situation or to other people, examine it. See what evidence it might turn up.

Take Advantage of the Venue

I once played mixed doubles with the chairman of a Fortune 500 company and his wife. Throughout the match he berated her and blamed her for every point they lost. Though she was no Martina Navratilova, he was no Bjorn Borg himself and lost at least as many points as she did. But he was simply incapable of admitting a mistake, and she was the most convenient scapegoat. If he missed a shot and blew the point, he blamed her for distracting him or asked why she hadn't put away the shot just before it. This told me something about what to expect when dealing with the man in business.

People often reveal their innermost selves in the most innocent of situations. How they deal with a waiter or an airline attendant can provide a fascinating glimpse beneath the surface. Knowing how impatient they are in a particular situation, or how upset they get over a minor error, can prove invaluable later on.

Recently I negotiated with the head of the governing body of one of the major international sports. On numerous previous occasions I had observed both his low impatience threshold and how he behaved once he lost his temper—which was to treat the entire situation as an irritant to be waved off, not to be thought about anymore. I knew if we patiently and politely stuck to our position he would eventually become irritated enough to dismiss the crux of the negotiation as a minor matter, which is exactly what he did.

Business is a constant process of keeping your own guard

up—in fact, it is the only way to do business—while encouraging others to lower theirs. Usually, the less formal the situation or venue, the more likely people will be to let their guards down. You will be surprised how much you can learn from a quasi-business or social-business situation.

I am a great believer in breakfast, lunch, and dinner meetings for this reason. If it is a new business relationship, I am often just as interested in observing the other party as I am in any business that may be discussed.

I was once having lunch in New York with someone I had not met before but knew from previous phone conversations that we were likely to be negotiating with one another. When the menus came, he told me he was on a strict diet and was going to have only a cup of coffee. This was a fairly prominent restaurant, and I found it interesting that he was not intimidated into ordering something just for the sake of ordering it.

But when the waiter came and I asked my guest out of politeness if he was sure he wouldn't have just a salad, he said, "Maybe I should," and added, "I'll have whatever you're having."

I found this even more interesting. If he could change his mind so easily, I had to wonder just how firm his "final" position in a negotiation might be, how easily influenced he would be to follow the lead in any negotiation—and even whether he might make concessions based on convenience rather than convictions.

None of this, of course, was to be taken literally. But I did think I had gained some insight that might prove helpful in my dealing with the man in the future.

Fish-out-of-water venues—or any small gathering in which people are forced to interact and operate outside their own comfort zones—can also be educational. I am constantly mixing diverse groups of friends, clients, and business associates for this reason. I find it instructive, for instance, to see how some of our sports clients respond to people from the world of business.

This, in part, helps me determine the degree to which I

should expose clients to customers and licensees prior to a commitment. Some—Arnold Palmer, Gary Player, Jackie Stewart, John Newcombe, and Jean-Claude Killy come immediately to mind—you can "take anywhere," and their personality is a key part of our sales effort. But others, if they aren't talking about themselves or to someone in their field, have nothing to say.

Observe Fringe Times

Formal business situations, highly structured meetings, negotiating sessions, and other forms of business interaction are likely to be the least revealing because these are the times when people are most likely to have their "game faces" on.

So consciously tune in to the fringe times, the beginnings and endings, the periods of transition, which are when people are most likely to let their guards down. During a two-hour business meeting, the first several minutes—before you actually get down to the business at hand—and the last several minutes—as everyone is saying goodbye—can tell you more about the people you are dealing with than almost anything else that goes on in between. These are, unfortunately, the times when you are likely to be least observant. Try to sharpen your awareness.

Also, be aware of people during interruptions, unusual exchanges, or anything that intrudes upon the more formal flow of a business situation. There is a certain amount of role playing in most business encounters, and when someone "breaks ranks" the facades are going to crack a little. Simply noticing who does the breaking and how others respond with words and eyes can tell you a lot.

There is a scene in *The Godfather* that perfectly illustrates this:

The Godfather has just flatly rejected an offer from the

Mafia boss to get involved in the drug business, when Sonny, his hotheaded eldest son, blurts out that the terms that have been proposed are insulting to the family.

This, of course, leads to the attempt to eliminate the Godfather. The other dons have correctly perceived a break in ranks, for simply by the act of objecting to the terms, Sonny has revealed a greater willingness than his father to consider the deal.

Though *The Godfather* is fictional, its psychology is very real.

Golf Course Insight

I am passionate about the game of golf. I have played it most of my life and have spent more time than I should trying to figure out what I find so intriguing about getting a small white ball into a small dark hole.

Part of the reason, I'm sure, is the range of emotions a round of golf can bring out and the complex array of personality traits it reveals.

I have often said that I can tell more about how someone is likely to react in a business situation from one round of golf than I can from a hundred hours of meetings. Maybe golf cuts more directly to the psyche than other games and situations. Or maybe it's the venue itself—green grass and rolling hills. It's astonishing how so simple a game can reveal so much.

The Gimme Putt

A "gimme" (give me) is a short putt conceded to the golfer by his playing partner or opponent. It's interesting to observe the broad behavioral spectrum relating to this tiny aspect of social golf.

Some people refuse all gimmes, insisting on putting everything in the hole and accurately recording the results.

Business translation: It's hard to do a favor for people like this.

Others don't even wait and assume it's a gimme—even if it's six feet from the cup. These are usually the big egos who, if they stopped to think about it (which they never do), would figure they could "command" the ball in the hole anyway.

Business translation: They won't ask you for a favor either; they *expect* it.

Most intriguing to me are the people who "half try" to sink the putt, sort of sweep at it one-handed. If it goes in, fine; if it doesn't, they "weren't really trying" and count it as a gimme.

In business, these people are hard to pin down. They have a capacity for self-deception, tend to exaggerate, and may give you a rounded off version of what they orginally said.

"What Did You Shoot?"

I've played golf a number of times with the CEO of a major corporation. When he's had a bad round he always shoots the same thing: "I had a seventy-nine." Of course, that seventy-nine includes a few post-gimme putts (after they rimmed the hole) and a couple of memory lapses in counting up strokes. What's interesting is that he really *believes* he shot a seventy-nine.

This kind of individual makes me nervous in a business situation. He has a capacity for creatively interpreting facts, then sticking to them until they become gospel.

"What's Your Handicap?"

Most people will be reasonably accurate about their handicap. But some will inflate it, maybe even double it. These are the people who want to con you, the ones who won't enjoy the round unless they take your money. That's also the way they will probably want to do business.

Others will tell you their handicap is less than it actually is. These people are trying to deceive the world about how good they actually are. They tend to dismiss their bad performances: "I'm having an off day today." How many times have you heard *that* in business?

Winter Rules

Winter rules—improving your lie in the fairway—are invoked when the fairways are in bad shape. It's kind of funny how wide the fairways can become for some people, particularly if there's a tree in the "fairway" between their ball and the green. No great psychological insights needed here: These people cheat!

The Rules of Golf

A course's local rules—or how the rules of golf apply to that specific course—are clearly stated on the back of the scorecard. What's amazing to me is not so much the interpretations that some golfers give to local rules but the mental contortions they go through in getting there. I'd much rather deal with someone who says, "See that white out-of-bounds marker over there? Screw it," than I would with someone who is still explaining his interpretation to me three holes later.

Watching People/Reaching People: My Seven-Step Plan

Obviously, there aren't 7 steps or 70 steps or 700 steps to learning to read people by opening up your senses. That's the whole point: If it were that categorical it could be learned in a classroom. Nevertheless, what I *can* say categorically is that learning to read people involves a few basic fundamentals:

Step 1: Listen Aggressively

Listen not only to what someone is saying but to how he is saying it. People tend to tell you a lot more than they mean to. Keep pausing—a slightly uncomfortable silence will make them say even more.

Step 2: Observe Aggressively

Have you ever said to yourself when watching a talk show or a news interview, "Oh, that person's nervous," or "Aha! That question made him uncomfortable"?

You don't need to read a book on body language to interpret certain motions or gestures or to "hear" the statement someone may be making simply by the way he or she is dressed.

Step 3: Talk Less

You will automatically learn more, hear more, see more—and make fewer blunders. Everyone can talk less and almost everyone *should* be talking less.

Ask questions and then don't begin to answer them yourself.

Step 4: Take a Second Look at First Impressions

I usually go with my first impressions, but only after I've carefully scrutinized them. Some sort of "thinking out" or contemplative process has to take place between your initial impression and your acceptance of it as a tenet of a relationship.

Muhammed Ali once said to me, "I'm more famous than Jesus Christ" (a line he perhaps borrowed from the Beatles). I was appalled at the statement, dismissed it as braggadocio, and let it go at that. But months later for some reason I got to thinking about it and started counting up all the Moslem, Hindu, and other non-Christian countries in which Ali was extremely well known. The statement was still braggadocio, but I realized it was also possibly true.

Step 5: Take Time to Use What You've Learned

If you're about to make a presentation or a phone call, take a moment to think about what you know and what reaction you want. From what you know of the other person, what can you say or do to be most likely to get it?

Step 6: Be Discreet

Discretion is the better part of reading people. The idea of using what you have learned properly is *not* to tell them how insecure you think they are or to point out all the things you have perceptively intuited that they may be doing wrong. If you let them know what you know, you will blow any chance of using your own insight effectively.

You don't owe anyone an insight into yourself for every insight you have into him. Remember, you can only use what you've learned if he's learned less about you.

The surest way to let people in on your own security quotient is to tell them all about your accomplishments. Let people learn of your qualities and achievements from someone else.

Step 7: Be Detached

If you can force yourself to step back from any business situation, particularly one that is heating up, your powers of observation will automatically increase. When the other person gets a little hot under the collar, he or she is going to be more revealing than at almost any other time. If you come back with an equally heated response, you will not only be less observant, you will be revealing just as much about yourself.

I am practically a missionary for the importance of acting rather than reacting in any business situation.

Acting rather than reacting allows you really to use what you have learned. It allows you to convert perceptions into controls. By reacting, by failing to step back first, you are probably throwing this powerful advantage away.

If you don't react you will never *over*react. You will be the controller rather than the controllee.

2 | Creating Impressions

IN 1964 I WAS walking down a street in Seattle with Bob Hope and Arnold Palmer when a woman came up to Hope and said, "Do you remember me? We met two years ago in Cincinnati." Hope was very polite but obviously had no idea who the woman was. After she left he turned to Arnold and me. "Can you believe that?" he said. "You meet 10,000 people a year and someone comes up to you two years later and expects you to remember her name."

As for me, I am pretty bad with names, and I presume everybody else is pretty bad with names, too. No matter how many times I have met someone, if I am not 100 percent sure that person knows my name—first and last—I am going to open with, "I'm Mark McCormack."

This is a minor point. But that's exactly what making the right business impression is all about. The day-to-day flow of business rarely provides for the Monumental Act or the Grand Gesture. Just as you can gain some of the greatest insights into people by the little things they say and do, it is the little things you say and do that often make the most enduring impression.

How people relate to you in business is based on the conscious and unconscious statements you make about yourself. The way you dress, your phone manner, your efficiency, the way you phrase a letter, the way you greet people all affect the impression you make on others—their "reading" of you—making people perceive you in the way you want to be perceived.

It is an artful form of manipulation. One of life's big frustrations is that people don't do what you want them to do. But if you can control their impressions of you, you can make them *want* to do what you want them to do.

In any new business situation there is a kind of mutual sizing up that goes on between the players. Each is trying subtly to exert his or her influence over the other. Whoever is better equipped to control the impressions being formed will walk away accomplishing the most, certainly in the short term and most likely in the long term as well.

A friend of mine calls this flash point of human contact the "pyrotechnics of business." While I can agree with this terminology in terms of the importance and impact of creating impressions, it may belie the subtlety of the process.

Obviously, people who think they are being manipulated and controlled won't be. The most effective executives impress in unobtrusive ways. Sometimes this is a simple act or gesture that, if never made, would probably never be missed; that's precisely why it will be noticed when it is made.

Often, particularly in negotiations, the way something is phrased totally alters the dynamics of the relationships involved. I have even seen it come down to the addition or deletion of a single word or two, the use of an "I agree," for instance, even when you don't, and before canceling it out with a "but . . ."

I was once having lunch with Ray Cave, the managing editor of *Time* magazine, and when we reached the restaurant Ray greeted the maitre d' with "Good to see you *again*."

The maitre d' perked right up and immediately led us to our table. After he disappeared, I said to Ray, "I thought you told me you had never eaten here before."

"I haven't," he said.

A colleague of Ray Cave, Patricia Ryan, the managing

editor of *People* magazine, once told me that if she is having a business lunch in which she anticipates being intimidated or not being taken seriously enough she will order a Scotch and water. She rarely drinks, but just ordering a Scotch instead of a Perrier creates a subtle, almost imperceptibly different, I-mean-business impression.

The subtlety of making impressions demands self-awareness—knowledge of the impression you create and the impression you want to create. Often people who think they are being impressive, who make a show of it or of themselves, are indeed creating very strong impressions, almost all of them bad.

But even worse than a skewed self-awareness is none at all. Have you ever seen a business executive, discovering there is a problem with an airline reservation, start to yell and scream at the ticket clerk? Here is the one guy left with the power to get that executive on that plane, and he goes out of his way to alienate him.

This is the own-worst-enemy syndrome. Even if you have something worth saying, expressing it in a tone or a manner that is a turnoff guarantees no one will listen.

Be aware of all the subtle opportunities you have every day for impressing positively and all the not so subtle opportunities you have for impressing negatively. Creating the right impression can be as simple as treating people the way they want to be treated. Or as difficult as treating them that way even when they beg not to be.

The impression you've made is what allows you to be less than perfect. If you can take advantage of all the little opportunities to create an overall, ongoing impression of competence, effectiveness, maturity, and fair-minded toughness—the kind of person people want to do business with—they will overlook the occasional transgression. People will forgive all sorts of "out-of-character" behavior in you if their overall, lasting impression is favorable.

Play Off Preconceptions

Consider doing the opposite of what someone expects. Often it's remarkably effective.

If someone is expecting toughness, it is amazing what a simple, self-effacing remark will do. If someone anticipates a hard line, making an immediate insignificant concession is a good way to begin. The more someone thinks I want something from him, the more I will go out of my way to appear as if I don't.

Recently we very much wanted to sign a reticent client, a well-known television personality who knew how badly we wanted to sign her and was expecting us to pull out the stops. In two get-acquainted meetings I told her a little about myself and our company and talked a lot about her career, her opportunities, and how, if I were in her shoes, I would go about taking advantage of them.

I never even mentioned the subject of representation. Naturally she began to wonder why we weren't pursuing her more aggressively—and she began to pursue us.

If I am presumed to be knowledgeable about a situation, I will often say something within the first minute or two of a meeting that might indicate otherwise. At the very least it is disarming, and generally, the less knowledgeable one appears, the more forthcoming and revealing the other party will be.

Conversely, if I am thought to be in the dark, I will drop one or two innocent comments that let the other person discover that I know more than he thinks I do.

In international business dealings, I have seen the language barrier—or a perceived language barrier—used effectively in this manner. *No comprende,* and its hundreds of linguistic variations, is a very useful business tool.

Americans, who are probably less conversant in second and third languages than almost any other nation (and are often defensive and insecure about it) are particularly vulnerable to language barriers, and foreign executives routinely take advantage of this fact. The American businessman who artfully drops one or two perfect phrases in the other person's native tongue may find that he's won a useful advantage.

Culture and customs are interesting even within the various regions of the United States. A born and bred New Yorker, for instance, doing business in the South is often vulnerable to what he perceives to be his own hard edge, and I have seen many Southern businessmen skewer "Yankees" on their own vulnerability. Whenever there is a perceived cultural contrast—big city versus small, entertainment industry versus Wall Street—there is probably an advantage for someone.

I have seen some people play off their own culture and customs. We deal with a very successful sports promoter in Japan by the name of Atsushi Fujita, whose methods, on occasion, can be somewhat unconventional. Several years ago, Mr. Fujita was representing the Japanese television rights to the Rose Bowl when one of the Japanese networks made an offer directly to the Rose Bowl Committee. When Mr. Fujita learned of this, he drove over that night to see the network's chairman and took his daughter along. Standing on this gentleman's doorstep and clasping the hand of his young daughter in his own, Mr. Fujita told him that if the network offer was not withdrawn he, Mr. Fujita, would lose face in America. Two days later Mr. Fujita had the Rose Bowl back.

Letters As Emissaries

Correspondence—both internal and external—is one of the most frequent opportunities you have for presenting yourself to the business community.

I'm a real stickler about any written communication that goes out over my name. I insist that it be neatly typed ("pleasing to the eye") and contain no spelling errors or typos. There are few things in business that you can easily make stick, but this is one of them.

It frustrates me to hear a secretary say, "It's *almost* right." Correspondence forms a strong subliminal impression about how you run your business, and I don't want someone to think I run it "almost right" when I have such a simple, obvious opportunity to impress otherwise.

I try to take the time to personalize all my business correspondence—with anything from a couple of sentences to a couple of paragraphs—to refer to some personal interest of the recipient's which has little or nothing to do with the subject of the letter.

This can mean bringing up a recent business deal that I know has gone his way, acknowledging his interest in a local sports team ("How about those Browns?" or "Did you get to the game on Sunday?"), or asking something about his family. It can mean expressing support—hoping that his workload has eased up or that he will finally get the break he's been looking for.

It is particularly impressive to personalize an initial solicitation letter. It's bound to get noticed because it will invariably raise the question, "How did he know that?" which will show, if nothing else, that you've taken the time to do some homework.

I also keep extensive lists of business Christmas cards and Christmas gifts, which I send out every year. The fall and holiday seasons are our busiest time, as they are with most businesses, and so every year it would be easy to convince myself to skip it, that no one really cares and probably won't even notice. That's what a lot of people do, and that's precisely why I don't.

Because they are so outrageously impersonal, form letters are awful. I don't think I've ever heard anyone say, "I received a great form letter today." The only thing worse than a "Dear Sir" letter is one in which your name has been carefully typed (usually spelled wrong) in a space provided, with the signature in fake ink! Have you ever seen a printed signature that looked real?

With the advent of the memory typewriter, I don't understand why form letters still exist. Yet they do, a monument to the triumph of bad form over possibly good content.

Marking an envelope "personal and confidential" for no real reason guarantees you a strong and immediate negative impact. Deception never makes a very good first impression. If you have to resort to using "P&C" to get someone to read your correspondence, you are probably doing a number of other things wrong as well.

Under the right circumstances, speed attracts. Telegrams, telexes, and cables get more attention than letters sent through regular mail. They carry an aura of importance that results in their generally being delivered immediately to the addressee rather than diverted to a secretary. The same can be said for Air Express, although this has become so common it's lost much of its impact.

You're Known by the Office Company You Keep

As we have seen, your secretary is your official link with the outside world, and how she deals with it is a mirror image of how the outside world sees you. If she is abrupt, you are perceived to be abrupt. If she drops confidential information, you are perceived to drop confidential information. If she drops names on your behalf, you are perceived as a name dropper. If she is officious and overbearing, then you are thought to be officious and overbearing.

The secretary of a leading British television executive consistently makes it impossible for me to arrange any sort of meeting with her boss. On countless occasions I have tried to arrange a get-together "at any time during the next two weeks" only to have his secretary tell mine that he is always "too busy." Yet without fail, when I get to the man directly, meetings are easy to arrange.

Of course, secretaries do play a certain protective role. By screening you from others, they enable you to act rather than react to a variety of business situations. However, there is a whole range of positive and negative ways in which this screening can be done. It is often as simple as the difference between saying, "Who may I say is calling?" and "Who's this?"

Secretaries often come off as drill sergeants, and I've seen executives who are amused by their abrupt manner and even encourage it. I suspect that those executives think that the abruptness makes them appear that much more important.

Of course this applies to all subordinates. If they work directly for you, it is likely that you are being judged at least partially by how they present themselves. So if you become aware of obvious rough edges, it is in your self-interest to point them out.

Dress As though You Mean Business

MCA/Universal was legendary for its severe dress code—dark suits and white shirts (its executives were sometimes greeted by "Here come the penguins"). What's interesting is that Lew Wasserman, their CEO, was *not* a stickler for formality—far from it. But he was running a fast-growing corporation in a highly volatile industry. And he knew that "Hollywood types" were invariably perceived as cigar-smoking hucksters who tend to stretch facts and round off the square corners of a deal. So the MCA dress code impressed in two ways: It created a positive image of stability—while dispelling a negative one.

The way you dress forms an immediate, strong impression about who you are. In general, it makes more sense to be dressed conservatively. If you accept that you can tell a lot about people by what they're wearing, it's safe to assume they can tell the same things about you. Obviously, the more conservative your business dress, the harder you are to read. People who show up for business meetings wearing loafers with no socks, their shirts half unbuttoned, and gold chains visibly exposed can evoke disturbing generalities about their entire personalities.

Several years ago we hired an executive who came to work the first day wearing nice gray slacks, an open silk shirt, and a conservative blue blazer. I asked his division head to explain to him that his dress was inappropriate for the office.

Many of our clients are in their twenties, and many of them, particularly the tennis players, show up for meetings dressed casually. But many of these twenty year olds are also millionaires, and we handle their money: We collect it, we manage it, we invest it. They want our executives to look more like bankers than like tennis players, even nicely dressed ones.

Coco Chanel once said that if a woman is poorly dressed you notice her dress and if she's impeccably dressed you notice the woman.

I think she could have given that same advice to business executives—male and female. As a general rule it is desirable to have your business dress say nothing about you—other than perhaps that your clothes fit.

Split Some Seconds

Whenever I'm involved in a new business relationship, I create situations that allow for split-second efficiency on my part. I will set up a phone call for 10 AM and will call precisely at 10 AM. I will promise to have a letter on somebody's desk by next Monday, and that letter will be there by next Monday. I will show up for an appointment exactly when I said I would.

Do this the first few times you deal with any new business associates, and they will assume you conduct all your business affairs that way. Moreover, they'll play along. You will find you will get the same on-time responses from them that they have come to anticipate from you.

Don't Be a Time Thief

The most frequent executive complaint is lack of time— enough hours in the day to get everything done. Yet these same executives become a lot less aware of time when it's someone else's.

The quickest way to make a lasting negative impression is to waste someone's time: use it cavalierly, or take up more of it than you need.

If you don't have something to say, don't set up a meeting just to make a contact. A contact who is really worth having will respond to your "I just wanted to meet you" by making sure you never meet again.

Don't make people waste their time in your office. It is exasperating to have to sit in someone's office while that person takes prolonged telephone calls. What is even more exasperating is to endure the chatty call that could have been easily handled with "I'm in a meeting. May I call you back in a few minutes?" If you *must* take a phone call when you have someone in your office, excuse yourself, then keep it short.

There are three exceptions to telephone behavior: when you are training a subordinate and you want him to hear your telephone technique or to learn firsthand about the facts of a particular situation; when you decide that the call might be germane to the meeting at hand; and when the person you are with might be favorably impressed by the person who is calling.

In the early 1970s Vice President Spiro Agnew, whom I had met once or twice, was trying to reach me about my representing the literary rights to a golf short story he had written entitled, "I Can Play Better Than This, But I Never Have."

I had tried to call him from my Chicago hotel but he was unavailable, and his office had asked where he could reach me. I had said that I would be either in the hotel or in the office of A. C. Spectorski, editor at that time of *Playboy* magazine.

While my meeting was going on in Spectorski's office, his secretary buzzed him and said, "The vice president of the United States is on the line for Mr. McCormack." Although the call had nothing to do with the business at hand, our meeting took on a whole new aura of importance.

Your Own Turf

There are times when one of the best sales techniques in the world is simply to "show up"—to hop on a plane and go wherever you have to go to meet someone at his convenience, at his office. Sometimes this is dictated by protocol, sometimes by a sense of the situation.

But as a general rule you are far better off having meetings at your own office rather than someone else's. This has very little to do with "power offices" and everything to do with territorial imperative. Even if all you have is a "power cubicle," it is still best to meet on your own turf.

First of all, it is *your* theater. You can exercise control over a meeting in your office that you simply don't have elsewhere.

Second, because of the territorial imperative, a meeting on your turf brings with it a sense of "invasion" by the other party. There is tension there, however sublimated it may be. Simply by being polite and making the other person feel comfortable you can diffuse that tension and earn a certain amount of confidence and trust even before the meeting begins.

The only office affectation I allow myself is keeping my lights very low. Otherwise, to me, a "powerful" office is either a very big one or one that is neat, clean, and efficient, a place where one can tell that business gets done.

Mean What You Say

Dow Finsterwald, former PGA champion, now head pro at the Broadmoor in Colorado Springs, once asked me for a favor. He had seen a print of a Leroy Neiman painting of him playing with Arnold Palmer, and he asked if we could get him a signed edition for his clubhouse. I called one of our executives who dealt with Neiman on a regular basis. He said there would be no problem, and I conveyed this news to Dow.

A month later I called that executive—I was in Japan at the time—and began telling him in so many words how, early in my career, I had promised to do something for someone and hadn't done it and how it had come back to haunt me. As I continued, it became clear that the executive had no idea what I was talking about. But as I approached the end of my story he blurted out, "Oh my God, the Neiman print!" We shipped it off a week later.

Business promises are made all the time, and almost as often they're broken—needlessly creating a horrible impression. If you *say* you're going to do something, *do it*. If you can't do it, think it's more trouble than it's worth, or don't want to do it, then *don't say you will*. Make up any excuse, but don't even say "I'll try." At the very least that leaves the other party with the impression that you tried—and *failed*.

If you say you will return a call the next day and you don't, that's enough to influence an entire relationship. There's no business law that says you ever have to return any phone call; just don't say you will.

It is also unwise to put yourself in a position of speaking on behalf of your company if you know there's a possibility, however slight, that your company won't back you up.

Many years ago, several people at Wilson Sporting Goods assured Arnold Palmer that if he ever wanted out of our contract with Wilson all he had to do was ask. Years later, when Arnold's association with Wilson had begun to deteriorate, I decided to test those assurances. Arnold and I were having lunch with Bill Holmes, Wilson's president, and I asked Holmes, "If Arnold wants out of the contract with Wilson, can he get out?" Holmes nervously replied, "The answer is no."

That incident was a great education for both Arnold and myself. We'd assumed that an individual was speaking for the company because he worked for the company. Arnold's disenchantment with Wilson led ultimately to the dissolution of his contract.

Promising someone you'll deliver something in a week and getting it there a month later is worse than not having promised in the first place.

Making a Notable Gesture

Business gestures are acts made on behalf or at the request of someone *for the purpose of obligating that person in some way*. Both parties may not even be aware of this purpose. You may like a business associate and genuinely want to do him or her a favor, but it is the obligatory nature of the business gesture that separates it from a personal one.

Again, subtlety is crucial. The more a favor is perceived as "owing you one," the less effective it will be.

I have dealt with executives who seem to keep a running tab of favors owed and given. Actually, I don't mind dealing with people of this sort. The point is to do them favors but never ask for one. The "score" is so important to them, they will eventually go out of their way to create opportunities for you in order to "get even."

Business gestures fall into three distinct categories: gestures that are easily overlooked, ignored, or misconstrued; gestures that are appreciated in passing; and gestures that are appreciated in the long term.

The first category obviously takes in all the gestures that either go unnoticed or actively work against you. There are certain gestures, such as making a call on someone's behalf or helping out one of his associates, that the other party may not even know about. You can't expect people to be appreciative if they don't know why they should be, and it is in your interest to let them know casually when you have made a nice gesture on their behalf ("We gave some time to your assistant last week" or "I let so-and-so know how much we have appreciated all your help").

The blatant favor is another interesting first-case example. If it is too obvious, it can be too easily misconstrued (or correctly construed) and will carry with it a conscious sense of obligation. Blatant favors can backfire. There are countless times when we are asked to get some shirts or golf clubs or tickets for someone and the color or size is wrong, the swingweight not quite right, or the tickets not very good, with the result that more bad will is created than if the whole exercise had not been attempted in the first place. It is kind of like trying to save the drowning man, breaking his arm in the effort, and then getting sued.

"Good intention" favors (such as gestures made on someone's behalf but without their knowledge) also fall into this category. Your good intentions may not always be in the other person's best interest, and this will either irritate him or go unappreciated, which will irritate you.

The second category often has to do with time—making the time to see someone, taking someone to lunch when the same amount could be accomplished in a five-minute conversation, taking the time over the phone or in a letter to express personal interest or concern.

One of the best "long-term" favors you can do for someone is to act as someone else's middleman—putting together two parties in whom you have no immediate interest. *Both* parties will remember.

The most important point about any gesture or favor, big or small, long-term or short-term, is that if you promise you are going to do something, either do it or let the other party know why you were unable to do it.

It is in these quasi-business areas that people seem to have the longest memories, and the overlooked or unfulfilled promise has a way of building on itself. Years may go by until one day, out of the blue, the person you disappointed will bring it up as though it happened yesterday.

Following are acts and gestures that will be appreciated, acknowledged, and over the long term, eventually returned:

Do Something for the Kids

Sometimes the most impressive gestures are indirect. When my son Todd was in grade school, he was crazy about football. A business associate of mine arranged for Todd to meet the Minnesota Vikings' quarterback, Fran Tarkenton. Todd was absolutely thrilled—and *I* never forgot it.

If you have a client or customer you want to impress, do something for his kids. It will mean far more to your customer than almost anything you could do for him.

What do you know about the families of your most important business associates? Have you ever expressed interest or taken the time to find out? It is information that can be well worth knowing.

Five or six years ago the aforementioned Mr. Fujita learned

that one of his business associates, an executive with Japan Air Lines, had a daughter who was a great tennis fan and idolized Martina Navratilova.

Recently, Mr. Fujita was promoting a women's tennis tournament in Tokyo, and still remembering this little fact, he called the executive who had since become head of JAL in Europe. Martina Navratilova would be participating in his tournament, Mr. Fujita told him. Would the executive's daughter like to come to Japan and act as her personal guide? The daughter accepted immediately—and her father could not have been more appreciative.

There is no better way to become closer to Japan Air Lines, and there is nothing whatsoever inappropriate in the exercise.

Let People Off the Hook

People often agree to do things and then for a variety of reasons beyond their control are no longer able to do them or may even no longer want to do them. Circumstances may have changed; new information may have altered their desire to make the deal, or they may have been overruled by someone higher on the corporate ladder.

As a lawyer, it's easy for me to treat a commitment as a commitment and a deal as a deal. But I've often found that by recognizing extenuating circumstances and letting someone off the hook I have accomplished much more for myself and my company in the long run.

For a number of years our consulting company had a contract with Wilkinson Sword. During the mid-1970s Wilkinson went through a rough period, and Chris Lewinton, its managing director, came to me and said, "Mark, we are in some difficult times and I am going to have to ask you, as a favor, to let us substantially reduce the retainer we are paying you."

Without hesitating, I indicated that would not be a problem.

In the following years, when Wilkinson was back on its feet, they not only increased our fees to make up the difference but when they were later acquired by Allegheny International the relationship was expanded further.

The corollary to "Let people off the hook" is "Let them change their minds." There's always a temptation to come back with, "But you said" or "But you promised." If you can take a moment to listen to *why* someone wants to change his mind and then place it in the perspective of the overall relationship, you may find it in your best interest to let him.

Drive a Soft Bargain

Expanding on an existing business relationship is almost always easier than starting a new one. By creating the right impression you make people want to deal with you over and over again. Achieving that often comes down to knowing how hard to push.

I have a close friend and business associate named Kerry Packer, who, among other things, owns Channel 9, Australia's largest commercial television network. Several years ago David Frost, also a friend of Kerry's, called Packer to try to sell him Australian rights to his upcoming Nixon interview tapes. Frost had spent a lot of money on this project and was urgently trying to recoup his investment.

He told Kerry he wanted $175,000 for the tapes, but Packer replied that for Australian rights alone he would not go higher than $160,000. The two of them argued back and forth over the phone and really weren't getting anywhere. An impasse like this, particularly between friends, can often end in disaster.

Finally David, in a moment of candor, said, "Kerry, I really *need* the $175,000. And I'm sure the tapes are worth it."

Packer was silent for a long moment. Then, he said, "I've

got an idea, David. I have a coin right here. Let's flip for the difference. You call it."

Frost, on the other end of the phone, coughed nervously and hesitated. "All right," he finally answered. "Heads."

"You win," said Packer.

Where does your self-interest lie—in a short-term gain or in a long-term relationship? Sometimes you can make the best deal for yourself by driving a soft bargain.

Flatter Legitimately

False flattery is transparent and can easily backfire.

But legitimate flattery—appreciating and acknowledging someone's genuine business skills from which you have benefited—can be quite seductive. If you think someone has acted "smart" and you have benefited from it, tell him how smart you think he is. (But don't call someone smart just because he bought from you. This falls in the category of false flattery and raises suspicions rather than trust.)

One of the most effective forms of legitimate flattery is to make the person you are flattering look good in the eyes of others in his company. Several years ago, when Noel Morris was the CEO and managing director of Slazenger in Australia, I tried to tie the longevity of Gary Player's and Jack Nicklaus's contracts to his tenure as CEO. He was flattered that Player's and Nicklaus's interests and fortunes were so directly tied to him, and it didn't hurt us to have someone at Morris's level directly looking out for our clients' interests. As it turned out, the Slazenger board would not approve this, but both objectives were accomplished anyway.

Make Friends

All things being equal, people will buy from a friend. All things being not quite so equal, people will *still* buy from a friend.

Make friends.

You don't have to become bosom buddies with everyone with whom you do business. But call them up occasionally, find out what they're doing, chew the fat—express interest.

It is important in our business to call a client and ask him how he played over the weekend or whether he's sorted out a problem with his second serve, his sand wedge, and so forth. It's so simple to do, and yet sometimes even people in my own company tend to forget what these seemingly insignificant phone calls mean to personal relationships. So did I until I learned the hard way:

After we'd been around a few years and were representing Arnold, Gary, and Jack, I knew full well how good our company was and how much better we were than any other alternative a pro golfer could find. It was completely obvious to me that if any golfer wanted the best job done he would seek *us* out.

What I failed to realize was that many of the new golfers coming up were not aware of the scope of the services we offered or the full extent of our talents. And if they were, our sit-back attitude and our failure to stroke a few egos came across as both cold and arrogant.

We didn't take the time to go out on the tour and make friends. A few other people did, and during the 1970s a lot of the best young golfing talent signed with other managers.

If you're not going to make friends, resign yourself to dealing with neutrals and enemies.

And if you are not going to keep friends, you had better be miles ahead of the competition.

Make Mentors: Make Confidants

Both mentors and confidants can lead to very effective business relationships. Both will want to buy from you, want to help you out, want to do you a favor whenever they can.

"Mentorism" is simply a matter of seeking advice and direction from someone you trust and respect. Pretty soon, the line between giving you this advice and doing you a favor totally disappears.

Making a confidant does *not* mean betraying confidences or giving away corporate secrets. It means sharing your personal feelings from time to time, passing on information that doesn't affect you but may be helpful to him, or encouraging *him* to confide in you.

I knew that David Foster, the former chairman of Colgate, enjoyed one-upping his ad agency, particularly when it came to Colgate's heavy involvement in golf sponsorship. I'd feed him whatever information I could pick up on the pro golf tour, and as often as not he would know of opportunities in this area before his agency did. It was harmless enough, but it served the very real purpose of helping Foster keep his agency slightly off balance.

We did a lot of business with Colgate.

Be Discreet

I don't think there is any way I can overemphasize the importance of confidentiality in business. People may like what you're telling them, but on a deeper, more subliminal level—the level of trust—they don't like the act of your telling them.

If one of our tennis executives tells Chris Evert Lloyd all about what Martina Navratilova is up to, Chrissie can't help but wonder, "What is he telling Martina about me?"

It's this simple: If you violate a confidence, the act will eventually come back to haunt you. It is one of those business lessons that everyone, it seems, has to learn the hard way. But you only have to get caught once. The result is usually so embarrassing, so humiliating, and so unnecessary that the lesson sinks in.

One of our financial executives was once talking to Virginia Wade about certain activities of another client. Virginia, who can be a little mischievous, really tried to draw out more information and was pretty successful. Later on, however, concerned, she told me about the incident and urged me to have someone speak to the executive in question. We did and now he's much more circumspect.

We have a rule in our office that when you mention a client's name in a letter you must presume that the client is going to see it. If a letter goes out saying, "If you can't have John Madden, how about John Havlicek?" I guarantee you that somehow both Havlicek and Madden are going to find out about it.

Even if you think you know where someone's loyalties or self-interests lie, don't assume that a request for confidentiality will be honored and don't commit it to paper, period.

Even when you have nothing to hide, discretion is still the better part of business valor. We once had a major client who had a very volatile relationship with an outside mentor/advisor. In the down periods, this client would always tell us he was getting rid of his advisor and would ask us what we thought. On one occasion we made the mistake of telling him.

We misjudged the influence of the other person and in doing so antagonized him so much that it seriously jeopardized the relationship we had with our client. We would have been much better off saying nothing and remaining neutral.

Indiscretion and breaking confidence always leads to problems that, in retrospect, you can't believe you created for yourself.

The Most Important Personal
Asset in Business

Obviously the real answer is common sense. But if you don't have it already, you probably never will, and there's nothing I can say here that's going to change that.

Common sense aside, then, the most important asset in business is a sense of humor, an ability to laugh at yourself or the situation.

Laughter is the most potent, constructive force for diffusing business tension, and you want to be the one who controls it. If you can point out what is humorous or absurd about a situation or confrontation, can diffuse the tension by getting the other party to share your feeling, you will be guaranteed the upper hand. There are very few absolutes in business. This is one of them, and *I've never seen it fail.*

John Kennedy probably understood it as well as anyone. He diffused Congress and an always hostile press with a sense of humor when, at times, that was all he had going for him. No president since Kennedy has ever really figured that out.

A sense of humor creates one of the most favorable long-term impressions. A single humorous, self-effacing comment can immediately let someone know that you don't take yourself too seriously, and that is the sort of thing that people remember.

It is also the best way to start a meeting. You don't need to have them rolling in the aisles, but a mildly pleasant remark at the outset will create the right atmosphere for everything that follows.

Finally, humor is what brings back perspective, which, next to profits, is the easiest thing to lose in business.

Many years ago the Ford Motor Company went through a period in which the numbers people literally took over the company and were closing plants left and right in order to cut costs. They had already succeeded in shutting down plants in Massachusetts and Texas and seemed to be relishing their newly found power.

Robert McNamara, who was president of Ford at the time, called a meeting of his top executives to discuss a recommendation he had received for the closing of yet another plant. Everyone was against it, but the predictions from the accountants were so grim that no one was willing to speak up.

Finally a salty Ford veteran by the name of Charlie Beacham said, "Why don't we close down all the plants and then we'll really start to save money?"

Everyone cracked up. The decision was made to postpone any more closings for a while, and the bean counters went back to working for the company rather than running it.

Being Yourself

Everyone has, or should have, certain principles by which he or she lives and conducts business. But more sins are committed in the name of "principle" than in almost any other I can think of.

"Principle" is too often a convenient cover-up word for bruised ego. There are a lot of insensitive, insulting people out there, and I think there are occasions when it's perfectly acceptable to take certain actions in the name of bruised ego. But don't call it principle if it isn't. That's a dangerous form of self-deception.

Speaking of deception, there's a big difference between playacting and miscasting yourself. The difference should be obvious, but if there's ever any confusion over when to play a role and when to be yourself, stick with the latter.

Obviously a great deal of role playing goes on in business. If you consistently present your "up-front-warts-and-all" self, you're not going to be very effective. The key is to come across as your best self by playing a role that features your strongest business qualities and hides your worst.

The classic own-worst-enemy cases are those people who don't know the difference between honesty and tact. Everyone's heard the twist on the cliché, "Honesty is not always the best policy." I think that's misleading, implying that sometimes in business it's okay to lie. It is more appropriate, and more accurate, to say, "Honesty can be mitigated." The truth can be couched in such a way that it is neither insulting nor self-destructive.

The other extreme is being too anxious to please. I have seen people playing a role "get on a roll." Pretty soon they are saying things they can't possibly back up and promising things they can't possibly deliver. Once you can't deliver what you promise, you are perceived as lacking authority, and the ultimate impression you end up creating is one of weakness.

Emotion Management

None of us has the luxury of doing one thing at a time, and it is very easy to allow the emotions attached to one activity to spill over into another. If a big deal has just fallen through, it is hard not to convey some feeling of disappointment to the next person you talk to. Or if you are feeling particularly harassed, impatience or irritation can often creep into a phone call or meeting.

Compartmentalizing, leaving the emotions of a particular situation locked within the confines of that situation, is one of those things that is easy to advise and very hard to do. I have found that a partial solution is to compartmentalize my day and week functionally—answering letters in the morning, returning phone calls in the afternoon, limiting meetings to particular meeting days, and so on.

It is also important to force yourself to act rather than to react to situations. For example, I rarely take calls, but I always return them. You are much less likely to snap at someone on the phone if you are initiating the phone call than if you are being interrupted by it.

In the end, compartmentalizing is mostly a conscious process of putting some emotional distance between yourself and the situation.

You Don't Have to Be Perfect

It is not very popular these days, or even politic, to claim that you know John DeLorean, much less that you ever did business with him. I do, and I did. DeLorean's sin was hubris, not incompetence, and the fact remains that anyone who was able to rise so meteorically through the concrete-hard bureaucracy at General Motors understood something about business.

I first met DeLorean when he was already head of Pontiac. During the course of a couple of meetings (he was an *instant* decision maker) I had more or less convinced him that Pontiac should associate itself with the U.S. Ski Team, with a commitment totaling seven figures. We agreed to meet several weeks later at Pontiac's ad agency, MacManus, John and Adams, in Detroit to talk about specifics and finalize the deal.

This is precisely the kind of promotional campaign that advertising agency executives hate. They knew that DeLorean and I had agreed to *something* but had no idea *what*. They weren't even sure how their agency fit in, if at all.

The day of the meeting arrived and I was primed. Here at one end of the table was the maverick from Detroit, one of the most powerful men in the automobile industry, and here was I at the other end, a young sports entrepreneur from Cleveland. In between were all these nervous-looking

MacManus executives, and *I already had the deal in my back pocket.* I was feeling invincible.

The whole tone of the meeting was set by 9:01 AM. The meeting had been scheduled for 9, and we were waiting for Ernie Jones, chairman of MacManus, to arrive. DeLorean looked at his watch and said, "Let's start."

By the time the conversation turned to the specific nature of the tie-ins between the U.S. Ski Team and Pontiac, I was totally winging it. After making several other suggestions, I launched into a fairly long soliloquy about some ideas I had for tying in the ski team with Pontiac's Indian head logo, which had been the company's symbol for many years.

As I talked I noticed that everyone's eyes had started darting back and forth, from me to DeLorean. DeLorean was totally impassive, but I sensed from the others in the room that I wasn't being as impressive as I thought I was and that maybe it was time to shut up.

After a moment of silence—in fact several long moments—DeLorean smiled. "Mark, you really researched the hell out of us. Pontiac's just spent a little over $3 million *getting rid* of the Indian head symbol and developing a new logo."

The deal went through anyway, but I don't think I've ever been so ill prepared for a meeting since then.

I once heard someone say, "Everyone makes errors. It's when those errors are repeated that it becomes a mistake." You don't have to be perfect, but you should learn from your imperfections.

3 | Taking the Edge

TAKING THE EDGE IS the gamesmanship of business. It is taking everything you know about others and everything you have allowed them to know about yourself and using this information to load the deck—to tilt a business situation slightly to your advantage. It is winning through intuition.

In the beginning it is a matter of doing your homework, knowing the players and all knowable aspects of the game. And in the end it is knowing how to play the game itself—figuring out what people want or convincing them of what they want and finding a way to give it to them. The idea, of course, is to give slightly less than you get in return.

I strongly believe that in any business situation there is an edge out there for the taking. Don't be greedy, don't be pushy, don't be impatient, but keep looking for the edge. Eventually it will show itself, and when it does be ready to do whatever you have to do to take it.

Know the Particulars

You can't take an edge until you have first taken a look at the facts. Facts alone won't guarantee you an edge, but they can protect you from handing it over to someone else. Unless you know all or most of the pertinent givens of the situation, you are dealing from a partial deck. Assume that the one fact you don't know—maybe because it's a little harder to find out—is the one that will make the difference.

There are many shortcuts in business, but this isn't one of them. Do the necessary spadework. Take the time and make the effort to learn everything you can about the companies and the people you are dealing with. The operative facts, the ones that define the situation, will start to present themselves.

There is a second set of facts which must often be intuited. These are the ones that arise out of the situation itself—things that people say and do which can provide new and useful insights. I have seen, heard of, or been involved in countless business situations where the emergence or the sensing of a single fact totally altered the dynamics or the tactics of everything that followed.

The first time I attempted to sell the American television rights to the British Golf Open Championship that is exactly what happened. I had been negotiating with the head of sports for one of the networks. When we met to close the deal, I brought along one of our top television executives, and he brought along someone from his "business affairs" department (networkese for lawyers and accountants).

Within minutes I knew the meeting would go nowhere. The head of sports, who was doing the talking, was not about to concede anything in front of his business affairs guy or to depart in any way—to "break"—from what the two of them had discussed prior to the meeting. The presence of my television executive, with whom they dealt more frequently, only exacerbated the situation. They did not want to appear to fold to any of my demands in front of him.

These were the operative facts that far outweighed all the others. It no longer mattered what I was selling or what they were buying or whether we kept talking for a week. This meeting simply wasn't going anywhere, and to try to make it would only pull it further apart.

As soon as I could, I suggested we end the meeting and take some more time to think about our positions. The next day I called the network executive, and away from the influences of others, we concluded negotiations for a rights agreement that has been in effect ever since.

Know the Players

The whole point in reading people, determining ego, finding soft spots, and so on, obviously, is to use this information to your advantage—by exposing what you know about someone to the right stimuli.

For several years I had been trying to convince Andre Heiniger, the worldwide chairman of Rolex, to sponsor the construction of a new electronic scoreboard and timing system at Wimbledon. He felt it was a waste of money, and he equated the sponsoring of time clocks at sporting events with the mass market watchmakers, the Seikos and the Timexes of the world.

I knew the only chance I had of ever changing his mind was to get him there, which I finally managed to do during the Wimbledon fortnight of 1979.

As we sat in the Royal Box, sipping tea and watching the match-in-progress, I could see him taking everything in: the antiquated elegance of the Centre Court stadium, the excitement of the match, the beauty and the charm of this very special place.

When the match was over, Heiniger turned to me and made a slow, sweeping gesture with his hand.

"This," he said, "is Rolex."

Size Up the Situation

Once you know the particulars and the players and have analyzed all the ramifications, you can start to size up a situation. Step back and see what opportunities exist at the outset.

I am a great believer in "stepping back," in taking a moment to place any significant business event—good or bad—in a larger perspective. I force distance between myself and events as a matter of business course and treat the need to do so no differently than the need to make phone calls or attend meetings. This may not be "teachable" but it is "learnable" because I have had to learn to do it myself. If everyone did this more regularly we might see the GNP jump overnight.

Several years ago I met a Venezuelan oil and shipping businessman by the name of Raphael Tudela. As I have come to know, respect, and admire him, he has impressed me as the quintessential street-smart executive. He has built a billion-dollar business from scratch in less than twenty years. He seldom deals in written contracts because his word is his bond. He has always made his own breaks. And his principal business, which is oil speculation, relies on his constant process of seeing opportunities where no one else does and taking advantage of them.

In other words, Raphael Tudela is a genius at taking the edge. One of the best illustrations of this—of how he has the facts, knows what people want, and figures out a way to give it to them—is the story of how he got in the oil business in the first place.

In the mid-1960s, Tudela owned a glass manufacturing company in Caracas, but, a petroleum engineer by training, he longed to be in the oil business. When he learned from a business associate that Argentina was about to be in the market for a $20 million dollar supply of butane gas, he went there to see if he could secure the contract. "If I could get the contract," he told me, "then I'd start to worry about where I'd get the butane."

When he—a glass manufacturer operating alone with no previous connections or experience in the oil business—got to Argentina, he discovered his competition was formidable: British Petroleum and Shell Oil.

But feeling around a little bit he also discovered something else: Argentina had an oversupply of beef which they were desperately trying to sell. By knowing this one fact—his first "edge," so to speak—he became at least an equal to Shell and BP. "If you will buy $20 million of butane from me," he told the Argentine government, "I will buy $20 million of beef from you." Argentina gave him the contract contingent upon his buying the beef.

Tudela then flew to Spain, where a major shipyard was about to close down from lack of work. It was a political hot potato and an extremely sensitive issue for the Spanish government. "If you will buy $20 million of beef from me," he told them, "I will build a $20 million supertanker in your shipyard." The Spanish were ecstatic and delivered a message to Argentina through their ambassador there that Raphael Tudela's $20 million of beef should be sent directly to Spain. Once again he had found the edge and taken it.

Tudela's final stop was in Philadelphia at the Sun Oil Company. "If you will charter my $20 million supertanker, which is being built in Spain," he told them, "I will buy $20 million of butane gas from you."

Sun Oil agreed, and Raphael Tudela fulfilled his desire to get in the gas and oil business.

Thinking on Your Feet

As a general business rule I am dedicated to the importance of acting instead of reacting—and so never over-reacting—to or within any business situation. The one ex-

ception to this may be the circumstance in which an edge
or opportunity must be taken advantage of immediately or
it will disappear forever.

The need to be opportunistic, to think on your feet, again
underscores the importance of tuning in to people—of hearing not only what they are saying but the larger and underlying meaning as well. This alone can tell you when taking
an edge is dependent upon an instant reaction.

We recently had a meeting in Chicago with McDonald's
for the purpose of renewing their commitment to the World
Triathlon Championship, which we produce and televise
for them.

As the meeting progressed, though no one really came
out and said it, we began to sense that they were much
more reluctant to renew than we had anticipated. For one
thing, they were less than pleased with the international
coverage. Furthermore, the timing of our meeting was
terrible. McDonald's had just recently committed themselves to constructing the swimming pool for the 1984 Los
Angeles Olympics, and this had preoccupied all their promotional thoughts.

Still, we could sense that there was in the room a mood
to buy—to commit to *something*—and who knew how long
that kind of momentum was going to continue? Probably
not a second longer than the meeting itself.

Out of the blue, our head of television sales suggested
that maybe the triathlon idea had run its course and that
what we really should be talking about was an all new yet
conceptually similar event: an international diving championship that would take place annually at McDonald's new
pool.

Because this one executive understood the ripeness of
the moment, instead of walking out with a failure we walked
away with a commitment.

How to Get Lucky

"Luck," the cliché goes, "is the residue of diligence." As Gary Player once said, "The harder I practice, the luckier I get."

Over the years we have had more than our share of luck. But over the years we have known how to take advantage of it—and we haven't waited for it to hit us in the face.

This, indeed, is the essential difference between those who are "fortunate" in business and those who aren't. The group that is "naturally lucky" can see the tiniest crack and turn it into a crevice. The group that "never gets a break" wouldn't see opportunity if it jumped up and down and then mugged them.

"Getting lucky" is mostly a matter of recognizing when you have been. Knowing then how to turn it into an edge is the easy part.

Consider the good fortune of Mr. Goodfather:

Mr. Goodfather (that's his real name) is a commercial horticulturist who waters and cares for the office greenery for a number of Cleveland companies, including Jones and Laughlin Steel. He learned that the Eaton Corporation, another big Cleveland firm—and a major customer of Jones and Laughlin—was moving to the same building, and he called Eaton to see if he could get their account as well.

When he asked to speak to the person in charge of the office, he was mistakenly connected to the person who was *really* in charge, Del DeWindt, chairman and CEO of Eaton.

"I take care of all the plants for Jones and Laughlin Steel," Mr. Goodfather said. "And I'd like to see someone about your account."

The next morning, Mr. Goodfather, wearing his work clothes and his trademark black beret, was ushered into a conference room to meet with several high-ranking Eaton executives, all of whom had their "Jones and Laughlin" files in front of them.

Once the case of mistaken identity was cleared up, everyone had a good laugh, and that might be the end of a cute, rather pointless story. But as Mr. Goodfather was leaving he turned to one of the executives and said, "Now, about your plants . . ."

He got the account.

Turn Crises into Opportunities

People tend to deal with crises only in terms of their potential for disaster. And yet in a crisis people are more on edge and agitated than they might otherwise be, and their vulnerability can be turned into a great advantage.

Recently a major, major client called up in a state of panic. One of the client's biggest licensees had decided not to pick up its option, which meant the potential loss of a seven-figure income and a great deal of exposure. The executive in charge of this particular client panicked also, and by the time I learned about the situation the executive had replaced the deal with an even better one.

That sounds like good news. But it just so happens that this particular client is paying us far less than we're worth. The client is a prestigious one for us and took advantage of that in working out our representation agreement.

Had our executive not been so quick to solve this crisis, I would have used the opportunity to explain some facts to this client: Yes, it was too bad about the particular licensee pulling out; yes, we felt we could replace it, but only by a great deal of time and effort and maybe by calling in a favor or two (which actually happened). I would have then brought up the subject of our fee, to see whether the client might consider paying us what we were worth in the first place.

One of the best rules I know is, when a crisis occurs or is in the process of occurring, *don't react*. Just say you'd like to think about it. Make any excuse, but don't respond. Once you have analyzed the crisis in terms of its potential for opportunity as well as its potential for disaster, then you can respond. This at least allows for clear-headedness in dealing with the problem, and if you're savvy about what's going on and haven't become caught up in the crisis yourself, it may present a very interesting edge.

Learn to Wait

People who deal with me often marvel at my capacity for handling bad news. This wasn't always the case, and though I haven't learned to *like* bad news, I have learned to deal with it. Bad news is seldom as bad as it first sounds, and most business disasters are rarely as disastrous as they first seem. Over the years I have learned—and am still learning—the importance of patience and how destructive the lack of it can be.

It is still amazing to me how the simple passing of time can totally alter a situation, solve problems, render other problems meaningless, cool down confrontations, and add a whole new perspective. "What goes around comes around" should be tattooed on the chest of every new, hyperactive executive.

What does this have to do with taking an edge? A lot. Part of being opportunistic is waiting, like a cat in a forest, for an opportunity to come along. Learning to wait, learning to be patient, has so many applications and ramifications it is difficult for me to give one or two examples without trivializing its importance. I would say, however, that in our twenty-odd years in business, 90 percent of our successes have involved in some way the need for patience, and 90 percent of our failures have been caused in part by a lack of it.

Recently we finalized negotiations of Herschel Walker's new contract with the New Jersey Generals, which in real dollar value is the largest contract in the history of team sports. The mere fact that we were the ones doing the negotiating is a testament to patience.

We were poised to sign Herschel two years ago, and after several meetings with Vince Dooley, his coach at the University of Georgia, we were convinced we would be successful.

In early 1983 I received a letter from Vince thanking us for our patience (!) and suggesting an appropriate time for a meeting with Herschel. I received this letter the same day that the news of Herschel's having signed a professional contract as an undergraduate hit the papers.

Our team sports division was devastated, but I suggested to them that we didn't know all the facts, that both Herschel and Vince were impressed with our approach to sports management, and that the contract he had signed was only for two years. I implied that with a little patience we might indeed hear from Herschel Walker again, and I strongly advised that this should not be the last he heard from us.

Herschel became a client twelve months later.

Discipline Yourself

There is a wide gap between the number of executives who are street smart and the number of executives who think they are. Those who account for this numerical discrepancy are often found languishing in middle and lower-middle management, usually blaming anything and anybody but themselves for their lack of advancement. The irony is that many of these executives are quite perceptive, even intuitive.

But their instincts are bad. What they pick up perceptively they always manage to misuse. Deep down inside they know what should or should not be said and when or when not to say it, but they can't help themselves. They blurt out some indiscretion, or can't check their need to "tell it like it is," even when they are aware that it is in their own worst interest to do so. This, of course, is business immaturity, and it afflicts as many people in their forties and fifties and sixties as it does in their twenties and thirties.

When a business situation must be handled discreetly, how do you rank your discretion? When a humorous or conciliatory remark might have taken the heat out of an exchange, how cooling was your influence? The next time you are ready to act impulsively, how good are you at resisting the urge?

How effectively have you used what you know about others, and how efficiently have you controlled what they know about you?

4|Getting Ahead

ONE OF THE BETTER Broadway shows of some years ago was a musical comedy entitled *How to Succeed in Business Without Really Trying.* The main character was a young employee who was constantly trying to impress his boss. In one scene he arrived at work a few minutes before nine, and proceeded to loosen his shirt and tie, muss up his hair, fill the ashtrays with cigarette butts, and throw papers and documents all over his office. When the boss arrived a few minutes later he found this employee "collapsed" at his desk, obviously comatose from working through the night.

It was a funny scene because, while it was obviously exaggerated, it dramatized the ridiculous lengths some people will go to in order to get ahead.

I have never had the "pleasure" myself of working my way up the corporate ladder, having gone directly from law practice into my own business. But I have observed friends in other companies who made it to the top, sports personalities who have parlayed athletic achievement into business success, and of course, our own executives, many of whom came to IMG by way of business or law school. I find the corporate structure just another venue for people watching.

Assuming similar backgrounds and capabilities, why do

some people shoot straight to the top while others seem to languish forever in the morass of middle management?

I think the overall answer lies in understanding the difference between *capabilities* and *effectiveness*, which is using those capabilities to achieve certain ends and results.

People who merely work up to their capabilities don't become stars.

Those who are stars combine their capabilities with other things—savvy, people sense, an understanding of how the game is played. They are usually achievers and can show results, but this is because they are effective in selling their ideas and themselves inside the company as well as outside the company.

One of our clients, John Madden, now a sportscaster for CBS, was for many years coach of the perennially successful Oakland Raiders football team. During those championship seasons, Oakland had an All-Pro receiver by the name of Fred Belintnikoff.

Madden once said about Belintnikoff, "If he had played up to his capabilities he would never have been in the NFL. He was slow, he wasn't very big, and he was even a little bit clumsy. I used to scream at him from the sidelines, 'Don't fall down, Fred! Don't fall down!' *All he could ever do was catch passes and score touchdowns.*"

Fred Belintnikoff was effective. He knew how the game was played, understood teamwork, and had figured out within the system the back doors and alleyways, *the personal moves* that would take him where the defense wasn't. He was a star at his position.

Know the Rules

Is climbing the corporate ladder a game? Absolutely. In fact, it is several games all going on at the same time. If you care about your career, you should take these games seriously and want to play all of them well.

If you're an employer, you should be constantly trying to recognize real talent and not to be misled by appearances. If you're an employee, you must figure out a way to let the true decision makers know how good you really are without making enemies of the people in between.

This can get complicated. You have got to be able to jump up several notches, to alert those several rungs above you to your talents. At the same time, you must make the middle guys think that by supporting you and building you up to the top guy they will look better as managers. You must also prevent these middle managers (who are looking out for their own interests) from stifling you or from appropriating your contributions as if they were indeed their own. Meanwhile, you must keep your peers as friends and maintain the support of your subordinates. It is not only complicated, it can also get pretty unpleasant and is one of the big reasons so many people become turned off by working for a company.

Getting ahead is one of those real-world concerns of everyday business life that no textbook can prepare you for. An M.B.A.—or a law or any other degree—can get you in the door. But once inside, you need to find a way to let people know your real worth. Can you look good without necessarily making someone else look bad? Can you play the game without playing politics?

The answer, I believe, is yes, but the first step is knowing the rules that make up the game, acknowledging the hardcore realities that influence relationships within the corporate structure. These realities vary widely from company to company, but three general rules come to mind:

Rule 1: Survival of the Fittest

Darwinism influences almost any pyramid-shaped structure, and the corporation is not only not an exception, it is probably the best example. There are simply not as many presidents as vice-presidents, as many vice-presidents as managers, and so on. This means that a natural antagonism, however subtle it may be, exists between different levels of management, different layers of the pyramid. A friend referred to it in his own highly politicized company as a "food chain."

Rule 2: Your Peers Are Your Natural Allies

It amazes me how often seemingly intelligent people are not very smart when it comes to recognizing this. If you alienate your peers, you won't need any other corporate enemies.

Rule 3: There Is Always a System

The "system" may not be very desirable or even work, but all companies have one. To get ahead you have to know your company's system and understand how to use it. That's the only way you can work within it, through it, or around it.

Making Impressions in the Long Term

Almost everything mentioned in Chapter 2 about making impressions applies to getting ahead, with one major addition: You are being judged internally over the long haul.

This places less of a premium on calculation and more on developing an ongoing support system of friends and allies. You can make a mentor outside the company with a few well-placed phone calls and occasional well-timed get-togethers. Mentorism inside the company is a week-in, week-out, month-to-month proposition.

The long haul also means that your big wins and your big losses—any single success or failure—are not nearly as significant as you may think they are. Have you ever heard anyone complain, "The whole attitude of this company is 'What have you done for me lately?'" I think that's a perfectly legitimate attitude because it is part of a trade-off: If you have a deal that goes sour or even several in a row, you don't expect to get fired for it. Conversely, if you ride the same winning horse for too long, people will start to wonder about the rest of your stable.

Being judged over the long haul also puts even more of a premium on patience, waiting for the right time to say or do something, knowing when to be visible and when to lay low.

Within the company, you are also more likely to be "found out." Your real self is likely to emerge, and your weaknesses as well as your strengths are likely to be discovered. As a result, you must realize that "you get along by getting along."

The Love-Me-for-Myself Syndrome

Some people are actually very good at what they do but take great pride in flaunting their weaknesses as well as their strengths.

We have one employee, a fairly senior executive, who is a very good manager. He motivates, his people are loyal, and he keeps an incredible number of balls in the air.

But he has two major weaknesses: He tends to meddle, and he talks too much. The annoying thing to me is that he is aware of both and seems to go out of his way to flaunt them. It's as though these were two perks that he's awarded himself. He's effective and will always have a job, but these habits limit him in other ways.

Practitioners of this love-me-for-myself (what-you-see-is-what-you-get) syndrome seem to view it as a mark of security when in reality it is very much the opposite.

Get Some New Tricks

We have an employee who is always snatching victory from the jaws of defeat. No matter what the circumstances, he acts as though it's the end of the world, as though only a miracle will help him pull this one out. And when he "miraculously" does, he believes this makes him look good to his superiors, as though the deal could never have happened except for his last-minute heroics.

We had another employee, who is no longer with us, who was always snatching defeat from the jaws of victory—or at least that was the way he made it seem. Every year his income projections would look incredibly promising, one year almost 100 percent above what it actually turned out to be. During the year, of course, this made him look as though he wasn't very good at what he did, as though he were screwing up half the time. But the cumulative effect over the long term was even worse. We began to discount almost anything he said or did by 50 percent.

Another bad trick I have encountered in our company are executives who literally "hoard" their clients or customers. Their overprotectiveness of these relationships indicates to me, as their employer, that they have little understanding of delegation, of how our company—and, indeed, most companies—is structured, or of the interconnections that make it work. While I may not question the sales skills of some of these executives, I question their aptitude for management.

I can think of a hundred more examples of this sort—

from the executive who always has some excuse that is so outrageous he figures it won't be challenged to the one who tells me that if I want him to be effective on the outside then I can't expect him to do what he is supposed to do on the inside. The point is that people working in a company tend to develop certain "tricks," or patterns of performance, which they believe place them in a favorable light with their superiors or make them seem indispensable to the company. Yet many of these patterns are so transparent and, over the long term, so predictable, that they tend to have the opposite result.

Since the nature and personality of one company varies from the next, I think the best way to find some "new tricks"—that is, tricks that work—is to observe people in your own company who have risen quickly through the ranks. In the rah-rah companies, for instance, you won't find any superstar who doesn't have some sort of that rah-rah zeal as part of his corporate persona. In our own company, which is really a group of twelve separate companies spread around the world, I place a high premium on intracorporate cooperation and communication. The executives who have gone the furthest are the ones who have figured out this "trick"—who can achieve their divisional goals within the overall goals of the company, who can make their division look good while helping other divisions to look good.

Step back and look at some of your own "tricks." You might find that what you think is promoting your best interest really isn't doing that at all.

Don't be predictable. You don't want to give someone above you the opportunity to say, "So-and-so is up to his old tricks again."

Three Hard-to-Say Phrases

Many people will say certain things because they wrongly assume they are creating the right impression and will equally wrongly avoid certain other statements for the same reason.

There are three hard-to-say phrases which I find myself saying quite often. In fact, most chairmen and CEO-level executives I've dealt with know how and when to say these three little phrases:

"I Don't Know"

It's amazing how many people are afraid of these words, who think that by using them they will somehow appear inadequate.

When I first shook hands with Arnold Palmer, I told him I could make only two guarantees. First, that if I didn't know something, I would tell him. Second, that when I didn't know something, I would find someone who did.

Today, I probably know more than I did twenty years ago, yet I find myself saying "I don't know" more and more all the time. I'll use it even when I really do know, sometimes to get more information or to compare versions of what is already "known," but mostly because I believe the self-effacing approach is almost always more effective than the know-it-all approach. Even when you have a definite opinion, it is often better to soften it by allowing for the possibility that you may not be omniscient: "I don't know, but it appears to me that . . ."

The inability of people to say "I don't know," even in innocent social situations, can give you an insight into their business character. I really do enjoy watching these people squirm sometimes as they try to bluff their way through conversations.

What these people fail to realize is that not admitting what you don't know can lead to suspicion about what you do know.

"I Need Help"

People are often afraid to ask for help or to accept it because they believe that somehow this will show that they are inadequate in their job. If they would think about it for a moment, they would realize that the system is set up for getting and receiving help. The whole corporate assumption is that certain tasks, and effectiveness in accomplishing these tasks, are sometimes better achieved by groups than by individuals. We have an executive who insists on being the "Lone Arranger." He won't bring in a deal, or involve anyone else in it, until he has it totally wrapped up because he is afraid he won't get all the credit. On several occasions both he and the company would have been far better off if he had asked for help and used some of the talent available to him.

Not asking is such a short-sighted and narrow-minded view. Asking for help is the way to learn, the way to expand your knowledge, your expertise, and your value to the company. It also demonstrates a willingness to work with others.

There are limitations, of course. Asking for the same kind of help repeatedly might indicate some sort of learning disability. Nevertheless, more often than not, particularly in aggressive companies, people tend not to ask for enough help rather than for too much.

Equally important is knowing, when asked, how to give help. Those who don't suffer from the same kind of deal paranoia that afflicts the Lone Arranger. People who are reluctant to share their knowledge, their contacts, their trade secrets with others within their own company are simply not going to have a very strong support system when they need one.

Your accepting help and your giving it are going to be remembered and acknowledged by any sort of enlightened management. There is nothing wrong with self-interest, even selfish interest. In fact, the best-run companies all seem to have a way of combining self-interest with corporate interest. But acting in a way that *sacrifices* corporate interest for self-interest limits your effectiveness and will be noted.

"I Was Wrong"

The chairman of a medium-sized company recently expressed to me his frustrations over the conservative attitude of his management-level employees. "The problem," he said, "is that they're all afraid to make a mistake."

There is a business philosophy I subscribe to which says that if you aren't making mistakes you aren't trying hard enough. I believe that to get ahead in business you have to be constantly testing the edge. This means that often you are going to be wrong. The good executives are right most of the time, but they also know when they are wrong and are not afraid to admit it.

The people who are least secure about their abilities have the hardest time admitting their mistakes. They fail to realize that making a mistake and admitting it—owning up to it—are two totally separate acts. It is not the mistake itself but *how a mistake is handled* that forms the lasting impression.

These people would be so much better off, and would look so much better in the eyes of management, if they could admit their mistakes and get on with it rather than waste everyone's time trying to rationalize them, cover them up, or lay the blame elsewhere.

I have seen some very capable executives get excited

about their mistakes. They feel that by doing something wrong they may have learned something right and can't wait to try again.

An ability to say "I was wrong" is essential to success because it's cathartic. It allows these successful executives to "get on with it," to put their mistakes behind them, and to move on to other things which may contribute to their next big success.

Trust

Obviously no employer would have anyone working for him whom he didn't trust. But I think in any company there are certain employees who are trusted more than others because their judgment and character are so solid.

From time to time I have had to deal with the problem of employees who tend to "fit" the facts into their version of reality, and tell less about a situation than they actually know or only what they want you to know.

It's interesting to me how consistent these people are. If I suspect someone of being less than totally forthright, I will have one or two of his expense reports sent to my office. Expense reports are like a truth serum.

Since I travel about 250,000 miles a year, I have a pretty good idea of what it costs to travel, and I would think this would be fairly obvious to those who work for us. Yet those employees I suspect may be playing it a little too coy are invariably the ones who tend to broad-brush their expense numbers, round them off to the highest zero, and apparently take taxis back and forth several times before arriving at their destination.

I don't always bring these expense accounts up right away but will often deal with them subtly at salary review time.

Reading expense reports is another means of reading

people. It is interesting to see which executives must always stay at the best hotels and eat at the best restaurants, even when dining alone. It tells you something about the kind of ego trip they're on. Also, in our business, where glamorous locales are more the rule than the exception, you can tell those employees who plan "business trips" around prearranged vacations and those who take some pains to avoid even the appearance of this.

People do not like to feel they are being conned, and no one is going to support the career of a subordinate who is a little too secretive, a little too clever for his or her own good. If you feel the only way to get ahead is to con the people you work for, then you'd better be very good at covering yourself because over the long term there are so many different ways you can be found out.

Loyalty

Loyalty is another form of trust. Employees often do not realize the importance almost any company places on it. They will trade off loyalty for a gain that is too small or a goal that is too short-sighted.

Obviously, if you believe another company is about to make an offer you can't refuse, you would be crazy not to pursue it. But if you do not intend to leave you have to be very careful about how to use other opportunities.

If people don't like to be conned, they don't like to be threatened either. Your *threat* of looking for another job only hurts you. You have, in effect, told your employer that you don't place much value on loyalty and, worse, that you don't even have anything to show for your attitude. You lose something important while gaining nothing. I have never been favorably impressed by someone telling me he is head-hunter bait.

If you *do* have another job offer but would like to remain

with the company you work for, *stress* the importance of your loyalty. Instead of saying, "Look, they've offered me this. Either match it or top it or I'm out the door," find out how much more effective it is to use slightly different words: "Obviously, this is where my loyalties lie. What can the company do so that I don't have to take this other job?"

C.A.D.I.F

Everyone has a boss, from the president of the United States, who can be fired every four years, to the chairman of the board, who must keep the stockholders or a parent company happy. And like it or not, your boss is judging you by these three criteria:

Commitment

If you feel anything less than total commitment to your job, don't let the boss in on your little secret.

Attention to Detail

The big screw-ups get aired and thereby psychologically exorcised. It's the little ones, too minor to mention—a report that can't be found, a failure to perform a little chore—which build up irritation and resentment.

Immediate Follow-up

As insignificant as this may seem, there is nothing that impresses so significantly.

Don't Use the Office to Make Your Personal Statement

People are so career-minded today this is less of a problem than it used to be. But it still angers me when any of our own executives use the office as some kind of personal forum.

This can involve any number of things, from the way someone dresses, to a refusal to accept or participate in a new system because "it's a waste of time," to setting his own hours, to catering to his own ego.

Self-assertion within the corporation is a very delicate thing. The trick is to conform—to know when to blend in—while sticking out at the same time.

Separate personal issues from corporate or substantive issues. Assert yourself only when the time and place are appropriate.

Don't Change the System; Work Through It

Companies never function according to their organizational charts. They are made up of people and personalities and politics and power plays, none of which can be connected by solid or dotted lines.

It is important to know the system so that you can work through it. Too many people spend too much time fighting against the system. The best and brightest spend their time learning how to use it.

Every company has its secret organizational chart, and the system itself is the best clue to figuring out what it is. Understand how it's supposed to work and you will begin to understand how it *really* works. Who are the decision makers? Who's hot and who's not? What are the shortcuts and where are the back doors? How do things really get done?

I don't think you have to play politics in order to get ahead. Have you ever noticed that the people who complain about office politics are always its victims? But I do think you have to make some friends. In fact, this is essential. In order to be effective you have to develop lasting relationships inside the company as well as outside. The bigger the company, the more important this becomes.

Again, see your peers as your allies, not as your competition. If you can hitch your wagon to a few of your company's brightest stars, you will climb right up the ladder with them.

On Making It Easy on Yourself by Making It Easy on Others

We had an executive in New York who was always complaining about our legal department in Cleveland. He maintained that the time it took to draft or sign off on his contracts was hurting his effectiveness. I knew the situation and he was probably right, but he failed to appreciate that our legal department had its own set of priorities and that he might not always be at the top of their list. In fact, by ranting and raving all the time he virtually guaranteed that he would not be.

One day the head of our legal department took this executive aside and said, "Let me show you how to work with your lawyer. The next time a contract comes in, review it yourself, and then, before sending it off, attach a covering memo that lists any problems you see and how you might recommend fixing them. Let's see if this speeds things up. If it doesn't, we'll try something else."

Needless to say, there was never a need to try something else.

When you need something from another department, ask yourself, "What can I do to make it easier for them?" If you need sales information, don't insist on speaking only to the sales manager; find out from him whom you can call. If you have a problem with another department, make sure they are aware of the problem before you demand an answer. Show people in other departments that you want to work with them instead of conveying the attitude that somehow they work for you. You will find that when you need that peer group support it will be there.

Pick Your Shots

The quickest way to lose credibility is to rage about minor offenses because of a buildup over major ones. This is the corporate version of getting a divorce because your spouse squeezes toothpaste from the middle of the tube. We're all susceptible to it, but it also shows immaturity and reveals lack of good judgment. Moreover, most companies don't have the time to psychoanalyze you to find out where the real problems lie.

When you join a new company at any level, the job comes with a certain amount of chips. Your judgment as to when—and over what—to use these chips will either add to your winnings or send you looking for another game.

Pick Your Spots

Your effectiveness in a company is directly proportionate to your ability to leverage yourself: "How and where can I make the most impact in the least amount of time?" Yet many people in business seem preoccupied by a fear of being left out. If a committee is formed they want to be on it; if a meeting is called they want to attend it. I once arranged to have lunch in New York with several executives whom I had not seen in a while. I later discovered this innocent get-together had become known as the "lunch committee," and several executives were actually upset that they had not been "appointed" to it!

Intracorporate cosmetics is an undeniable fact of corporate life. And while committees and meetings do contribute to corporate visibility, you have to pick your spots. Leverage your attendance at meetings and your appointments to committees. Look for those where you can gain the most and avoid those where you can contribute the least. When I see the same face popping up at every meeting, I start to wonder when that particular executive has time to get anything else done.

What Do You Do Beyond Your Job Description

The projects people take on which are not part of their day-to-day job description, which have not been assigned to them, are those projects for which people get the most credit and recognition.

The jobs most people have existed before they got there and will continue to exist after they've left. The job is the constant. What you do by going beyond it is what gets noticed. Most positions in a company are three-quarters functional, meaning the set responsibilities and duties that came with it, and one-quarter personal style. The degree by which you can stretch this 25 percent is the degree by which you will stand out in your company.

What Are You Doing Here and What Do Others Think You Are Doing Here?

Several years ago we gave one of our executives the new top-level position of chief financial officer of our overall group of companies. A month or so after the appointment, I called the executive about a fairly urgent matter and was told he was in Pittsburgh for the day seeing a Mr. Rogers.

Pittsburgh? I could not recall our having any banking or financial commitments in Pittsburgh. Mr. Rogers? The name didn't ring a bell, but we deal with hundreds of financial people, and it wasn't likely that it would.

When I spoke to the executive later that day he told me that his meeting with Mr. Rogers had gone very well. I asked him who Mr. Rogers was and he said, "You know, the guy who wears a sweater and has a TV program for kids."

I had to wonder what my chief financial officer was doing in Pittsburgh signing up Mr. Rogers. In fairness, part of the executive's former responsibilities had included the licensing of children's products and apparel. While I thought it was fairly obvious that his new position was a full-time job, apparently this had been less obvious to him.

This is a fairly extreme example, but the simple truth is that the vast majority of people working in your company have absolutely no idea what you do there and the rest are laboring under misconceptions. If you were to write out what you do for the company and your immediate superior were to write out what he thought you did for the company, you would probably be amazed by the discrepancy.

Why is this important? What difference does it make?

First, the classic corporate "failure to communicate" begins at this level. I once heard someone use what I thought was a wonderful line in describing the feelings that many people have about their companies: "Their insanity becomes your reality." If you and your boss are laboring under different assumptions about your goals and priorities, is it any wonder that you are often mystified by some of the decisions that get made and the failure of others to see what may be perfectly clear to you?

Second, on the more direct subject of advancement, you are probably being judged by certain criteria that would be news to you. And you are probably making certain contributions to your company that would be news to them, which is a big reason people fail to get recognition.

Compare notes with your boss. What does he think you are doing here, and what do others think you are doing here? Once you can agree on the givens, you will be less shocked by the assumptions.

Don't Go One on One with the Boss

If you win the battle you're probably going to lose the war. And the more right you are, the more damage it will probably do in the long run.

We had a situation several years ago where one of our employees got into a heated exchange with his boss. One thing led to another, and the employee was asked to resign.

This was a very unfortunate situation, and he asked to see me because he felt that once I knew all the circumstances of the dispute I might be willing to prevail upon his boss to reconsider.

I told the employee that I would be happy to listen but that there was nothing I could do because my larger priority was supporting the management structure of the company. No matter how wrong or intemperate his boss might have been, that, unfortunately, was now a nonissue.

The situation did not reflect well on this particular employee's boss—but his boss still had a job.

No-Wins

The people who buy new companies are rarely the people who have to go in and run them. But if you're the one they turn to for help, make sure you're not entering a no-win situation.

"We've Just Bought This Company and We'd Like You to Run It"

You can't stop your company from making stupid acquisitions or getting involved in businesses they shouldn't be in. But you can try to avoid becoming part of a team that's going to "continue its success" or turn it around. For more often than not you will find yourself in a no-win situation.

A company is usually bought for one of two reasons: Either it is successful, which means the best you can do is make it slightly better, or it is unsuccessful and the buyer feels he can turn it around.

There are always hidden reasons, as well as the obvious ones, as to why a company is unsuccessful. Sometimes you know all the problems and what can be done about them, but this kind of foreknowledge is rare. Usually it is not until you have already committed yourself and are in position that you discover the real problems and whether they are correctable. Moreover, if you have taken on a management position in a business you know nothing about, you start with one strike against you. Your efforts are going to be resented by employees who do know the business even if they aren't very capable of running it.

"It May Seem Like a Lateral Move But . . ."

Versions of this exist up and down the corporate structure. The lateral shift, particularly if you suspect the skills involved are not your strong suit, presents a two-pronged problem. Either the new division is already well run, which means you will never get any credit, or it's poorly run, in which case your effectiveness is probably going to be limited by those above you.

"We've Created This New Position Especially for You"

The job doesn't make much sense to you and you aren't really sure it will work in practice the way it sounds in theory, but the pay is better and it's more responsibility. . . . Watch out.

"This Job Really Requires the Special Talent of Someone Like You"

Beware of any position with a long list of dead bodies attached to it. It's best to talk to a few of those dead bodies before jumping into an open grave.

Get into the International Division

If I were offered any job I wanted in a company and I didn't know the company that well, I would ask to head the international division. All else being equal, this is where I could probably make the most impact in the least amount of time.

You can count on your fingers the American companies which are maximizing their full potential in international markets.

Of all the world's companies, American-run businesses are by far the most arrogant and chauvinistic. Most of their international divisions haven't taken the time to break down language and cultural barriers, preferring to declare them impenetrable to their managements.

There are eight billion people out there and less than 3 percent of them live in the United States. Get into your company's international division. You can go a long way just raking the cream off the top.

Burnout and Boredom

Psychologists would probably tell me I am a prime candidate for burnout: I work too hard and too long under extremely stressful conditions. Yet I have never experienced anything close to what must be a terrible psychological state.

I do, however, take precautions. I schedule time for exercise, relaxation, and rest, including naps in the office, and I observe those time commitments just as I would any other business time commitments. I have learned to compartmentalize my business emotions as well as my business day. I write everything down, and since I put my notes where they will pop up again in the right place at the right time, once I have written something down I forget about it. The end result is that when I break from work I break from work-related stress as well.

I think a far more pervasive problem than job burnout is job boredom. I've never experienced extended periods of boredom either, though like everyone else I go through a trough now and then.

Boredom occurs when the learning curve flattens out. It

can happen to anyone at any level of the corporation. In fact, it occurs most often in successful people who need more challenge and stimulation than do others.

One of the sure signs of incipient boredom is knowing your job to well, or knowing all the right buttons to push. I simply will not allow this to happen to myself.

I find that I am redefining my job all the time, taking on new tasks, or constantly creating new challenges for myself. If I reach some goal, either personal or corporate, that goal immediately becomes a step in the learning process toward another, more ambitious goal.

This, I believe, is how people grow in their jobs and grow in importance to their company.

If you're bored it's your fault. You just aren't working hard enough at making your job interesting. It is also probably the reason you haven't been offered anything better.

Find out what you love to do and you will be successful at it.

Since I still get up at four or five every morning and still put in eighty to ninety hours a week, even though I really don't have to anymore, one of the first things I am usually asked by reporters and interviewers, "Why do you keep pushing yourself so hard?"

I always wish I had a better answer to give them, but the simple truth is all I can come up with: "I love what I do."

What You Can Learn from Working in the Mail Room

You won't learn humility. You won't learn respect. You won't learn the company inside out or from the bottom up. What you will learn is something very important, and per- haps a bit frightening, about yourself.

The people who get ahead have a need, are driven to perform a task well, no matter what the task is or how mundane it may actually be. They bring to any job an attitude which actually transforms the job into something greater. Carpenters who become contractors at one time had a need to drive a nail straighter and truer than anyone else. Waiters who end up owning restaurants were at one time very good waiters.

Some executives, had they started in the mail room, would still be sorting mail—and misrouting most of it.

II
Sales and Negotiation

5 | The Problems of Selling

MOST PEOPLE, I BELIEVE, are born salesmen. At school we sell our peers on accepting us and our teachers on giving us good grades. We try to sell our parents on letting us stay out at night or use the car or buy a new stereo.

Unconsciously we are already employing many of the aspects of selling: powers of persuasion; the art of negotiation; and the ultimate teenager's tactic—"Never take no for an answer."

By the time we get to the outside world we have learned how to position ourselves to get what we want, how to market our abilities, and how to sell ourselves on job interviews.

Then something happens. We forget how to sell. We question our own sales aptitude. Suddenly the techniques we've used all our lives become foreign and mysterious, as though we now had to go out and learn them for the first time.

And yet the art of selling is the *conscious* practice of a lot of things we already know *unconsciously*—and have probably spent the better part of our lives doing.

The problem is that once we enter the real world of business a new factor emerges. For the first time our powers of persuasion, our sales abilities, are being judged. This can be intimidating, and so we respond by convincing ourselves that we can't sell, we don't know how to sell, or we don't want to sell. We then use these mental roadblocks to justify our lack of sales aptitude.

But the real problems of selling have little to do with aptitude and almost everything to do with how we perceive the process of selling itself. Some people find it beneath them; others find it intrusive. And almost all of us fear the rejection.

Selling Doesn't Seem Important Enough

One of the biggest problems that people have with selling is that it seems less important than it did twenty years ago. Historically the quickest way to the top was through sales. These days selling is perceived as one of the lesser business skills, conjuring up images of Willie Loman and the Fuller Brush man. People are more likely to believe that the quickest way to the top is through management training. There is some truth to this, but to presume that management skills obviate the need for sales skills is a dangerous form of self-deception. I have yet to meet a chairman or a CEO of a major corporation who didn't pride himself on his powers of persuasion—in other words, his salesmanship.

Selling is what they don't teach you at Harvard Business School. Business schools admit that their purpose is to train managers, thereby almost totally overlooking the fact that if there are no sales there is nothing to manage. This escapes a lot of newly minted MBAs, who in their desire to run a company may find sales, the techniques involved, the *art* of selling, beneath them.

We have had many MBAs work for our company, and I have found their lack of sales skills to be the biggest gap in their business knowledge. Fortunately, most of them learned to sell through on-the-job experience. But I have seen many MBAs at other companies who haven't, who persist in believing that an understanding of selling is not really a fundamental requisite of management-level personnel. This is sometimes called "lacking the common touch." I think it's more aptly described as lacking common sense.

I was amused recently by an article in the *New York Times* on Morgan Stanley & Company, the aristocratic investment banking firm which hires only the top MBAs. Morgan Stanley had beaten out twelve other firms in vying for the right to manage the Teamsters Union's $4.7 billion pension fund. Here's what the *Times* had to say:

> At one of their meetings with a committee of Teamsters trustees—union men and trucking executives— part of the session was devoted to the Morgan officers' individual backgrounds, with the emphasis on humble origins.
>
> One executive said that a scholarship put him through college. Another pointed out that he had joined the Marine Corps directly after school. And a third told the trustees sitting across the table that he had grown up in a modest household, the son of a railroad engineer. So it went as each of a dozen or more Morgan officials took his turn.
>
> "It was as if they said, 'I know we have this portrait of J. P. Morgan up on the wall, but we're really regular guys,'" said one participant, who asked not to be named.

Anyone who can convince the Teamsters that J. P. Morgan was, at heart, a union man understands the importance of selling.

Selling Is an Intrusion

People hate to impose, to make waves. Have you ever found yourself nodding in agreement to something with which you totally disagree? Have you ever thought about sending back an overdone steak, then changed your mind?

A feeling that selling is intrusive is not a problem. It is an asset. The best salesmen all seem to have a sixth sense about this. They can tell by the tone in someone's voice or the atmosphere in the room when the mood or timing is wrong. And either because they don't want to impose, or because they know that it is not in their own best interests to do so, they will not antagonize their customer by attempting to make a sale.

The old foot-in-the-door school of high-pressure, super-assertive techniques has gone the way of the dinosaur. These were never very effective techniques to begin with, but perhaps they were necessary fifty years ago, when a salesman was not likely to see or speak to a customer for another six months. Today in the age of modern communication and transportation, if you are being intrusive and have enough people awareness to sense this, there is no excuse for not picking a better time and coming back. You do, of course, have to be willing to come back.

Effective selling is directly tied to timing, patience, and persistence—and to sensitivity to the situation and the person with whom you are dealing. An awareness of when you are imposing can be the most important personal asset a salesman can have.

It also helps to believe in your product. When I feel that what I am selling is really right for someone, that it simply makes sense for this particular customer, I never feel I am imposing. I feel that I am doing him a favor.

Fear

Fear is the single biggest problem people have with selling: fear of rejection, fear of failure.

So much of selling a product, a service, anything, is selling yourself, putting your own ego on the line. And what are the odds? If you're pretty good, you're probably going to fail half the time. Rejection, as they say, comes with the territory.

Rejection in selling is rarely personal, but simply knowing this doesn't make it any easier to take. I have always found that it helps not to be too "adult" about it. Learning to accept rejection doesn't mean having to like it. Acknowledge your real feelings, and if those real feelings are irritation, frustration, or anger, admit to them instead of pretending they don't exist.

I've been rejected hundreds of times. Yet tomorrow, if I've put in the effort and if what I'm selling makes sense and if I get turned down, I'm going to be frustrated or angry all over again. Realizing that it isn't personal doesn't mean you shouldn't take it personally. If you don't, in fact, it may mean that you haven't put enough of yourself into the effort.

Fear of failure is another problem that people have with selling. Sales results are so tangible, so measurable in black and white, there is no place to run or hide.

But what many people don't appreciate is that fear of failure is one of the greatest positive motivators in business. If you aren't afraid to fail, then you probably don't care enough about success.

Bjorn Borg had a reputation for being an ice man on the court. But he once told me that on key points he was always terrified, that sometimes it would take all the courage he could muster just to put the ball in play.

This was true as well of Arnold Palmer, and I believe this very human quality had more to do with his enormous popularity than all the tournaments he won. His fear of failure was so strong because his desire for success was so great. And when he failed, when he missed a shot, you could see the pain etched on his face, and you knew he cared.

6|Timing

MANY IDEAS FAIL NOT because they are bad ideas, not because they are poorly executed, but because the timing is not correct.

Some years ago we were involved in trying to establish a pro golf circuit in South America. We encountered all sorts of unforeseen problems, ranging from sudden currency devaluation, which undercut our cash flow, to spiraling inflation, which made the costs of continuing the tour prohibitive.

Our timing couldn't have been worse, and it cost us a lot of money to find this out. But we know that South Americans love golf. And so we are convinced that one day, given the right circumstances, this particular concept will work, and when it does, I'm sure we will be the ones who will make it work.

A lot of salespeople are far too quick to write off a good idea simply because their timing was bad. If someone says no to a project or an idea, it is not always because he doesn't like the idea or the project. It may be simply that for economic reasons or for other internal reasons you don't know about it simply doesn't work for that particular person at that particular moment.

Yet weeks, months, even years later, you will hear, "So-and-so doesn't like that project," or "Such-and-such company has already said no to that," or "They don't have the money for it."

Go Back in Five Years

If you believe in an idea, and if you believe that the idea should make sense for a particular customer, go back again. I can't tell you how many times I've seen an idea bear fruit when it is presented again at a more auspicious moment.

The simple movement of a clock, the flipping of a calendar, can totally alter the dynamics of a selling situation and the receptivity of the buyer.

Shortly after Bob Anderson became president of Rockwell International, I suggested that he hire our company to produce an internal promotional film in which Anderson would visit various Rockwell sites and explain their role in the overall operation of the company. We had done this kind of thing before, and we knew it was an effective device for promoting a family feeling in multinational companies separated by great geographical distances.

"Mark," Anderson said, "I just took over this job from the man whose name is still on the door of this company. The last thing I should be doing now is commissioning a promotional film—but try me again in five years."

Almost exactly five years later, I did just that. And Rockwell is considering a commitment of the necessary funds.

The Secret Life of a Deal

Timing has any number of direct applications to selling. It can govern anything from the time span over which a sale is made, to when in a particular conversation to say something, to when under a particular set of circumstances to do something.

Timing itself is not pragmatic. It is not a precept or a set of rules that can be followed but a percept—sensory signals that are picked up by the brain and then applied to the selling situation.

When you combine the perceptory nature of time with all the timing intangibles of selling—how long an idea should germinate, when to make a particular phone call, and so on—correct or appropriate timing is almost always a judgment call.

What this means is that those people who seem to be blessed with an innate sense of good timing are really those people who are most sensitively attuned—to themselves, to their customers, and to the selling situation itself. Almost any deal, whether it's a simple transaction or a complex series of maneuvers covering several years, gives off its own unique sensory signals, which are there for anyone to pick up.

Listen to Your Common Sense

The objective facts of a sale—its nature, its complexity, the people to whom you are selling, and certain information you learn along the way—can tell you most of what you need to know about timing. Apply this information with common sense. Do the obvious when you should obviously do it, and don't do anything when you obviously shouldn't.

If your customer doesn't know you or your company, it is obvious that a sale will take longer than if he does. If the buyer is underwhelmed by your initial presentation, it's obvious you'd better take the time to exchange some ideas before presenting it again. If you know the buyer's selling-in process will take several months, don't try to force a commitment out of him after several weeks.

Recently I received a call from a company that was looking to buy a sports concept tailored to a very specific set of promotional needs. As it turned out, just the week before I had seen a concept from our tennis division which, with a couple of minor variations, was exactly what this particular company was looking for. (This, by the way, is an example neither of good nor of bad timing but of *fortuitous* timing, which is totally beyond the seller's control but which everyone deserves now and then.)

I told the person who had called that I would like to think about it, that I wanted to talk to some of our people, and that I would get back to him in exactly two weeks.

Even though I knew we had what he wanted, it was obvious to me that if our concept was to look inspired I had to allow some time to pass between his problem and our solution. If I called him back the next day, he would wonder just how much brilliant conceptual thinking had actually taken place. But by giving him a precise time when I would be calling, he would not only wait for the call; he would be anxious to hear from me.

A good general common sense rule of timing is: Don't blurt out anything. Take a moment to consider whether the situation demands a certain timing strategy or whether you can use timing to your advantage. If it doesn't, and if you can't, you can always call right back.

Listen to the Buyer

The salesman controls the timing of a sale, but he takes his cues from the buyer. Obviously this places a premium on listening rather than talking, on really hearing what the buyer is telling you rather than paying it "ear service."

You can pick up a lot of timing clues just by asking the right questions. Many companies, for instance, because of budgeting and other considerations, are more receptive to buying at certain times of the year than at others. This kind of information is usually available for the asking.

And if you know the buyer well, if you've taken the time to make him a friend, he will give you good timing cues— when to initiate, when to close, whom to call and when— throughout the selling process

Follow the Script

The timing of a sale can be as central to getting a commitment as what is actually said and done. If all the selling variables that determine timing had to be separately weighed and analytically considered, the correct timing "answers" to even the simplest transactions would require several computers.

Fortunately, your mind does this for you. It computes through sensory perceptions what could never be arrived at through analytical thought. Timing, then, is a matter of converting these sensory perceptions into conscious actions or conscious inactions (when *not* to say and do certain things).

This process is easier if you envision the time frame as the "life span" of a deal, or as separate from the deal itself, a third party to the transaction. Most deals seem to have a secret life which follows a kind of preordained script. Anyone who has ever "killed one" by closing too quickly or too late, by shortening or extending a sale beyond its "natural life," would probably attest to this.

A single selling situation may require anywhere from several seconds to several years. Obviously the more complex the deal and the more phases it has, the more important it is to picture this script in your mind, to attune yourself to a deal's separate or secret life. The timing for each phase— when and for how long—is already typed out like stage directions. Correct timing—converting sensory perception into appropriate conscious actions—is a matter of seeing the script and following it.

Many people, once they see the script in their minds, have an overwhelming need to depart from it. In their haste to make a deal, they want to compress the time frame or cut directly to act III. They want to rewrite the dialogue or eliminate the buyer's lines altogether. They see the signs for appropriate timing but ignore them and fail to massage the situation properly. By rewriting the script they give it an unhappy ending.

Instant Gratification

We are all pulled by the urge for instant gratification, and everything about the corporate environment seems to increase this urge. Get it out of the way. Go on to the next thing. One less ball up in the air means one less thing to worry about.

But even if we can make people do what we want them to do, we can rarely make them do it when we want them to. People and events move at their own pace and almost never go according to our own timetable. One of the surest signs of business maturity is an ability to postpone instant gratification, to adjust your own timetable to suit others.

As both a salesman and someone who runs a company, I can think of no aspect of timing that is more important than patience. Lack of patience alone is enough to blow a deal, while the application of it—letting someone ramble on philosophically while waiting out a particular situation—can singlehandedly turn a deal around.

I would guess that more deals are blown because of lack of patience than for almost any other reason. I see or hear examples of this almost every week:

• A salesman, on the phone, sensing the other party is harried or in an irritable mood, delivers his sales pitch anyway.

- A salesman, asked by a buyer to come back again, says, "But this will only take a minute."
- A salesman, while shaking hands on a deal, says to the buyer, "Now that that's out of the way, I've really got something to talk to you about."

If congenital bad timing is a disease, then patience is probably the cure.

Persistence

Persistence, as conventionally understood, implies that selling is strictly a numbers game, a question of how many doors you knock on and how many times you go back to knock again.

I doubt that this is the whole story in any sales business. In our organization, and I'm sure this is true of most service organizations, effective selling is as much a matter of the quality of the doors, and how and when you choose to knock, as it is of numbers.

But this is not to undermine the importance of persistence. Without the patience to wait and the persistence to go back again, any other insights into timing aren't worth very much. Persistence is certainly right up there among the basic sales commandments with "know your product" and "believe in your product."

Take Advantage of Timing Opportunities

There are any number of timing opportunities that drop in your lap. While you don't have to be a fortune teller to spot them, you do have to be sensitively attuned to their significance to tailor events to your advantage.

How to Extend or Renew a Contract

Extend, renew, or renegotiate a contract when the other party is the *happiest*, not when the contract is about to expire. Whenever we've done an exceptional deal for a client, I encourage the executive in charge to discuss extending the client's representation agreement then, even if it still has a year or so to run.

If a customer of yours has received terrific news, *even if it has nothing to do with your product*—a raise or a bonus, for instance—there's probably a good timing opportunity there.

Take automatic mood checks. Mood alone can turn a "yes" into a "no" and vice versa.

Take Advantage of the Bad Timing of Others

The bad or unfortunate timing of others can create all sorts of opportunities for you. You often see this in an election year, with each candidate being very cautious about when to throw his or her hat into the ring. Each is waiting for the others to make a political blunder so that he can then ride in as the white knight.

Just as you should renew a contract when the client is the happiest, sell one when the prospective buyer is unhappiest with your competition.

Our television division was recently seeking to represent world rights to a major sporting event. At the time these rights were controlled by one of the American networks. We learned, shortly after the event organizers did, that this network had recently sold a package of their lesser sports properties to a particular country, with the major sporting event included as the "prize."

The organizers were very upset to have been used this

way, and since they had already experienced problems with the network, I felt our timing might be pretty good: We now represent this particular event.

Weigh the Present Against the Future

When Tony Jacklin won the British Open in 1969, he was inundated by endorsement opportunities, particularly from England, which had been waiting a long time for its own golf champion. We felt, however, that Jacklin's win was no accident, and so we agreed only to short-term contracts, one year or less. A year later, Jacklin won the U.S. Open and his endorsement value tripled.

Conversely, when Ben Crenshaw first turned pro, I felt he had one of the most promotable images I had seen in pro sports. He was being touted as the "next Nicklaus," and while that is a nice reputation to have, it was next to impossible to live up to. I felt it was important to promote Crenshaw's image before it was associated with any success he might or might not have on the golf course. Unfortunately, Ben waited too long, and by the time we began representing him, the fact that he was something less than immortal hurt his marketability.

When Muhammed Ali was at the peak of his fame, the climate of the country simply was not as favorable for a black athlete as it was for a white one. It is now, and even back then you could see it was going to change. Had Ali worked on developing a positive, wholesome, "nonboxer" image, he could have made as much out of the ring as he did in it. But he never weighed the present in terms of the future, and his revenues from endorsements have never amounted to much.

Take Advantage of a Setting Sun

Pat Ryan, the managing editor of *People* magazine, told me
of a selling pointer that her father, the late Irish horseman
Jim Ryan, passed on to many of today's race-trackers. Always ask a prospective horse buyer around in the late
afternoon for tea or a drink. Sociability is not the point. The
fact is that there is no better moment to show a horse than
in the setting sun. His coat gleams; he looks full of life,
unbeatable. (This is the same reason that *Sports Illustrated*'s
bathing suit issues are always photographed at sunrise or
sunset.)

Few people are likely to require a sunset as a sales
backdrop, but it is a certainty that sellers can take timing
advantage of future events that are as inevitable as a setting sun.

One of our most successful television productions, "The
Superstars," which has been on ABC-TV for a decade now,
was sold in part because it responded to a certain timing
inevitability—the network's need to fill the winter sports
trough between football and baseball. The new football league
may change this, but for the present (and for the past ten
years) there has been an obvious predictability to this need.

The Calendar Is Loaded

Dates are what turn timing into concrete information. A
calendar, in the hands of the right salesman, can be a
potential sales weapon. In our business, for instance, we
know that, world politics aside, there is a certain inevitability to a 1988, 1992, and 1996 Olympics. We can begin
timing certain sales efforts toward these particular future
events.

Many of our sales efforts, in fact, are timed to take
advantage of major annual sports events, either to tie in

with them or to use them as a medium for customer entertainment.

Several years ago, when California's tax reform act, Proposition 13, was big news, I heard the story of how one gentleman, who was a professional lecturer on finance, took advantage of what the calendar told him about future opportunities. Several weeks before the proposition was to be voted on, he reserved a full-page ad in the *Los Angeles Times* which ran the day after the proposition passed. The ad, announcing his new lecture series, was headlined, "How You Can Profit from Proposition 13."

Coming In and Going Out

The best person to sell to is someone who has just arrived at a new company or is just leaving. When John DeLorean was leaving Pontiac he called me and said, "Mark, as soon as I get out of here, they're going to try to undo everything I've done. If you want to extend the Nicklaus agreement, we'd better do it now."

A newly arrived executive is anxious to do something, to make his mark, and he is usually given enough rope. An executive who is about to leave—and knows he won't be around for the headaches—doesn't care.

We've concluded deals because someone was tying up loose ends before he walked out the door and because he wanted to do business with us in his new job.

When Your Timing Is Considerate, Let the Other Party Know

For example, "I knew about this last week, but I didn't want to bother you during a sales conference (before the holidays, while you were working on your budget, and so forth). As a general rule, avoid making any phone calls (particularly if it's bad news or about a problem) on a Monday morning or a Friday afternoon.

Use (with Extreme Caution) Inconsiderate Timing

A phone call in nonbusiness hours, late at night or over a weekend, always has greater impact. If you're smart about it, you can use it to great advantage, but you'd better know what you're doing because it can easily backfire. Always set it up first: "This is so good (or so important) I'd like to talk to you about it over the weekend."

Don't Give Deadlines

Sometimes giving a buyer a deadline is unavoidable. But a deadline is a threat, and people who feel they are being threatened will go out of their way to call you on it. Deadlines should only be invoked as a last gasp measure.

The quickest way to lose credibility is to give someone an absolute deadline and then extend it, amend it, or ignore it. This is the corporate version of crying wolf. Once you've failed to observe your own deadline, everything else you say will be taken with a grain of salt.

Take Time to Soften a Threat

Timing can be used to soften the demand for a decision. If you doubt the sincerity of a "maybe," give someone a plausible time conflict which demands resolution.

I recently felt we were being strung along by a company that had originally indicated a definite desire to proceed.

The deal involved a major time commitment of one of the world's top-ranked women's tennis players.

Giving them a deadline would have been too threatening. Instead we indicated that if we did not have an answer within the next week it would become much more difficult and perhaps impossible for us to cancel some of her tournament commitments.

As it turned out, the answer was negative, but it was better to know this than to have it drag out indefinitely. By suggesting a time conflict we forced the issue without making it sound like take-it-or-leave-it.

Attention Spans

Busy people have short attention spans, so get to the point. Assume that you are there to listen and you'll talk less. Don't start with your life story; don't drag out a presentation; and unless you're a playwright, forget the dramatic buildup. All you'll succeed in doing is irritating people, or worse, making their minds wander. Also, learn the attention spans of the people you deal with. I know, for instance, in dealing with Bob Anderson of Rockwell that if I'm on any subject more than forty-five seconds his mind is going to be off on something else.

Shopping Lists

If you have more than one subject to discuss, or more than one idea or item to sell, make sure you reserve enough time for the most important of them. Never place yourself in the position of having to ask, "Could I have a few more minutes? I haven't gotten to my main idea yet."

Give Someone the Gift of Time

One of the best ways to impress a buyer is to take a half-hour of his time when he's expecting you to take an hour. One of the worst is to take an hour and a half.

7 | Silence

THE MEETING HAD GONE exceedingly well. We were in London, and one of our executives had just made an excellent presentation to some British businessmen. I was sure these gentlemen were quite impressed. A kind of dramatic silence occurred as they looked at each other to see who was going to respond first.

But just as one of them was about to speak, the executive began summarizing the positive aspects of the concepts he had just presented. This happened a few times.

Finally I actually laughed and said to him, "Ah, the joys of silence. . . . Let someone else speak."

A lot has been written about the use of silence in selling. For good reason. There comes a point in almost any sales pitch when the other person should be talking, and there comes a point in almost any sales pitch when *no one* should be talking. It's pretty hard to get to either point if you don't know when to be silent.

Silence has so many different selling applications. If you stop talking and start listening, you might actually learn something, and even if you don't you'll have a chance to collect your thoughts. Silence is what keeps you from saying more than you need to—and makes the other person want to say more than he means to. Knowing when to remain silent can strongly influence the impression you make on others. Furthermore, it's impossible to get a commitment out of someone if that person can't get a word in edgewise.

The tactical use of silence serves one of two purposes. It either lets the other person talk or forces the other person to talk.

Make the Other Guy Talk

I will often pretend not to know the specifics of a situation just to get the other guy talking.

Recently I was brought in at the tail end of a bitter renegotiation dispute. It had gotten pretty serious, and lawyers were sitting in on both sides.

Since I was the "new kid on the block," I asked the other party to start at the beginning and explain to me, in his own words, his understanding of the dispute.

He began to talk, and he must have talked without pausing for twenty minutes (I could see his lawyer wince several times). By the time he finished he had come around—or talked himself into—agreeing with much of what our position was.

Get Information by Not Asking for It

If you ask a question on a particular subject and the answer is unsatisfactory, the best response is none at all. If you are seeking more information, or a different kind of information, ask for it by remaining silent.

Silence is a void, and people feel an overwhelming need to fill it. If someone has finished speaking and you don't play along by taking up your end of the dialogue, after only the slightest pause that person will automatically start to elaborate. Eventually they may say what you want to hear.

Bite Your Tongue

A learned—it's almost never instinctive—ability to bite your tongue has two incredibly important selling applications that are often overlooked.

First, it allows you to collect your thoughts and therefore be more cautious or more circumspect in what you say. Second, it lessens your chance of saying a lot more than you need to, mean to, or want to.

It is common practice for a Japanese businessman with whom you are negotiating to use a translator even though he understands perfectly well what you are saying. It is a device that gives him more time to frame his reaction and response.

State the Positives, Omit Extraneous Negatives

I attended a meeting not too long ago with a business associate who was trying to involve a potential sponsor in a prestigious golf event, the Chevrolet World Championship of Women's Golf. After stating all the positives of this involvement (and getting a good reaction), he switched enthusiastically to the television coverage. Even though, he said, this event was opposite the Men's PGA Championship, both his company and the network anticipated very good ratings.

Even though it was opposite the Men's PGA Championship? I couldn't believe my ears. Granted, in our role as consultants, this is precisely the kind of fact that we would point out to our clients. But as a salesman I think this is precisely the kind of fact that one omits.

The important facts were the TV coverage and the anticipated good ratings, not a rundown of that day's TV competition. Even if my associate felt ethically bound to bring this up, his timing couldn't have been worse. He should have stated it at the beginning of the presentation, before all the positives, rather than ending it on a negative.

If you're selling someone a transistor clock/radio, I don't think you're obligated to point out that the battery will run down in twenty-one months or that a year from now there will be a better digital model on the market for less money.

State the positives and omit irrelevant or semi-relevant negatives. Be ethical, be moral—and be aware of the joys of silence.

The Pregnant Pause

The use of the pregnant pause in selling is very much like fishing with a net. You put some bait in a net and silently wait for a fish to swim in.

Once you get to the point in a sales pitch where you have asked for a commitment, *don't speak again* until the other person has replied in some fashion. Don't restate your case. Don't lobby. Don't tell him you know it's a tough decision, but . . .

The buyer may be struggling with his decision and conducting an internal dialogue with himself. Don't help him out. If he asks a question, answer monosyllabically.

Even if the silence is deafening, just let it sit there.

Once You've Sold, Shut up

I can't tell you how many times I've seen this happen: A sale is made and the salesman immediately raises suspicion by heaping hyperbolic praise on the buyer's judgment: "You won't regret this." "The best deal you've ever made." Even the most trusting person will start to wonder, "What have I just committed myself to?"

Once you've made the sale, anything else you say about it can only work against you. So change the subject. Talk about the buyer's golf game, his kids—anything but how extraordinarily brilliant he is for buying your product.

Even worse than the flatterers are the salesmen who insist, right then and there, on crossing every "t" and dotting every "i": "Great. Now let's go over these points again to make sure we are in total agreement." At best, this approach dampens enthusiasm. At worst, whole deals can become unraveled.

Confirm the Deal Later in Writing

In truth, particularly if the deal is complex or negotiated over a long period of time, there probably will be some deal points or details on which the two parties are still hazy. Don't get into them now. Confirm your understanding later in writing. It allows the meeting to end on a positive, upbeat note of good feelings, and it allows you to state in writing your version of these sometimes hazy details. Unless they are major points, or terribly wrong, these will usually become basic tenets of the agreement.

8|Marketability

MANY YEARS AGO I was having dinner with Andre Heiniger, the chairman of Rolex, when a friend of his stopped by the table to say hello. "How's the watch business?" the friend asked.

"I have no idea," Heiniger replied

His friend laughed. Here was the head of the world's most prestigious watchmaker saying that he didn't know what was going on in his own industry.

But Heiniger was deadly serious. "Rolex is not in the watch business," he continued. "We are in the *luxury* business."

To me, Heiniger's comment summed up the essence of "marketability." It is knowing what business you are *really* in and understanding the underlying perceptions that connect your product to the people it is being marketed to.

Ever since the passing of the Model T, the automotive industry has sold cars in terms of everything other than function—their power, sex appeal, luxury (where would we be without "rich, Corinthian velour"?), economy, and on and on. Automobile advertising, in fact, has historically been so persuasive that it has not only shaped perceptions but created them. It was once true, for instance, that a college professor would rather forfeit tenure than be spotted driving a Cadillac. If, on the other hand, a corporate executive chose to own a Volkswagen, one might seriously question if he indeed had the "right stuff."

Today's buyer, however, is more sophisticated than ever and is so hypersensitive to being "marketed to" that he may be turned off. This places an even greater premium on understanding marketability, which to me is the more subtle, underlying aspect of marketing.

Federal Express, for instance, may hard-sell its service, emphasizing speed, dependability, and size. But, as may be fairly obvious to anyone who had seen their commercials, what they are really selling is peace of mind.

One of the most subtle forms of marketability is building the perceptions into the product itself, doing everything one can to make the product "buyable." This "product," for instance—this book—if it were titled *Principles in Practical Management,* would certainly appeal to a different audience and probably, at least in terms of potential, a much smaller one.

Marketability cannot be "read out" from market studies, market tests, and focus groups but must be intuited. It involves looking at the fringes, looking just beyond them, and interpreting—*perceiving*—underlying motivation and why someone really cares or doesn't about your product. Marketability is further distinctive from marketing in that it is done, or should be done, before the fact, and if it is done correctly it doesn't cost anything.

Marketability is also the more active form of selling. Selling, by necessity, is product-oriented—features, functions, advantages, and so forth. But understanding your product's marketability puts the buyer into the picture, whether he or she is being sold to as the middleman (as in selling to a company) or directly as the consumer.

This chapter connects the two—product and people. It begins with product, and all the selling verities that affect it, and ends with positioning, or how what you say or show about a product can practically sell it for you.

Know Your Product, Believe in Your Product, and Sell with Enthusiasm

These are the fundamental selling truths. If you don't know your product, people will resent your efforts to sell it; if you don't believe in it, no amount of personality and technique will cover that fact; if you can't sell with enthusiasm, the lack of it will be infectious.

Nothing turns off a potential customer quicker than a salesman's lack of familiarity with his product. Have you ever walked into a department store, asked a clerk how a particular gadget or appliance worked, then stood by while he fiddled with the knobs and wondered out loud why they don't make things simple anymore? Even if he finally gets it to work, by that time your interest has diminished and you are not likely to make the purchase.

Knowing your product also means understanding the *idea* behind it—its purpose, how it is perceived—the *relationship* between it and what someone wants to buy. How will it help the customer? What problem is it solving? What is its promise?

An understanding of these intangible features is at least as important as knowing a product's mechanical features. Yet precisely because they are intangible, and may even vary from customer to customer, they are more prone to being misinterpreted and misunderstood.

Knowing your product also means understanding the image it is projecting. I believe all products project an image of some sort. It may be a positive one, which you want to promote, or a negative one, which you need to overcome.

The home computer industry, for instance, really didn't take off until it solved its image problem. Here was this device that saved time and simplified all sorts of tasks, yet it looked complicated and difficult to use. Until it was made to seem "friendlier," less forbidding, sales lagged.

Two Reasons I Wouldn't Buy from Me

Part of knowing your product is knowing all the reasons someone might *not* want to buy it. Anticipate the reasons. State them clearly in your mind, spell them out on paper if necessary—and have an answer ready for each of them.

A good portion of almost any sales effort is spent overcoming objections. Don't try to convince a buyer that his objections aren't valid. Concentrate instead on altering his frame of reference.

In anticipating and overcoming objections a salesman has to practice a kind of theory of relativity. He has to ask himself, "Compared to what?" Think about a major purchase you have made—buying a house, for instance—and the mental gyrations you went through to get there. At some point you were making comparisons. Compared to another house that interested you, but in a slightly less desirable neighborhood, it seemed expensive. Compared to what you could have bought it for ten years ago, it seemed outrageous. But compared to its resale value, compared to what someone else might have been ready to offer, compared to what you *deserve*, you were able to justify the price.

In licensing the name of an athlete, I know the two objections we are most likely to encounter are the price—the size of the guarantees—and the athlete's lack of availability to the licensors.

The president of a major apparel firm once told me that he wasn't going to pay an athlete more money than he was making himself. By this criterion, the seven-figure guarantee that we were asking probably did seem outrageous. But I was quick to point out that what he was buying was instant brand name identification, and compared to the tens of millions of dollars it would cost to develop a comparable degree of brand recognition, the guarantees were indeed reasonable.

He also questioned why, if he agreed to pay that kind of money, he was only entitled to five days of the athlete's time. Again, it was a matter of altering his frame of reference. From which would his company benefit more, I asked: additional department store promotions or this particular athlete winning more major tennis competitions? And didn't he agree that the best use of the athlete's time, as far as his company was concerned, would be hitting millions of tennis balls on his way to Centre Court at Wimbledon?

By helping the buyer see a different frame of reference, by altering his perceptions, we were able to finalize a licensee deal that has resulted in the company's most successful line of apparel and in several million dollars of income to our client.

Beating Dead Horsemeat

A dog food company was holding its annual sales convention. During the course of the convention the president of the company listened patiently as his advertising director presented a hot new campaign, his marketing director introduced a point-of-sale scheme that would "revolutionize the industry," and his sales director extolled the virtues of "the best damn sales force in the business." Finally it came time for the president to take the podium and make his closing remarks.

"Over the past few days," he began, "we've heard from all our division heads and of their wonderful plans for the coming year. Now, as we draw to a close, I have only one question. If we have the best advertising, the best marketing, the best sales force, how come we sell less goddamn dog food than anyone in the business?"

Absolute silence filled the convention hall. Finally, after what seemed like forever, a small voice answered from the back of the room: "Because the dogs *hate* it."

Sometimes an idea, a product, a concept is just plain bad. No matter how you flog it, no matter how you restate it, it simply won't work. The only solution is to walk away, to cut your losses.

Yet a lot of people try just the opposite. The more the evidence mounts that an idea may not be salable, a concept may not be workable, a product not desirable, the more determined they become, the more time they spend, trying to prove otherwise.

The 80/20 Rule

Since I have devoted the first third of this book to the importance of knowing your customer, it should be apparent how I feel about this.

The sales efforts of most people and companies follow the 80/20 rule—80 percent of your business is done with 20 percent of your customers. It makes sense to focus four-fifths of your time and effort getting to know the one-fifth of your customers who are the most important to you.

Many years ago we were hired by Wilkinson Sword in England to do a sports and leisure-time profile of all their key customers. Once the survey was completed we customized a series of sports outings, personalized to the customers' recreational tastes. The boxing fans and their Wilkinson counterparts were taken to a night at the fights with Henry Cooper, the European heavyweight champion at the time, acting as their host; the golfers played golf with Tony Jacklin; the cricket fans attended a pre–test match breakfast with the Australian cricket champion Ian Chappell.

Focus on the interests, predilections, and tastes of your top 20 percent, and take the time to figure out what you can do to keep them there.

Know the Company

There are two key points to knowing your customer's company. First, that knowledge can tell you something about the best overall approach. Second, though the person you are selling to may have total authority and autonomy, you are ultimately selling through him as the company's representative, to the company itself.

Companies can, and should, be "read" just as people can. The methodology, in fact—forming gut impressions based on raw perceptions—is almost the same. Watch the way a company does business, how fast it has grown, and the way it has chosen to position itself in the marketplace. Size and longevity alone can be indicators. Obviously one does not sell to an IBM the same way that one would sell to an Apple, or to an AT&T the way one would sell to an MCI. The approach, ranging from a mature, conservative one to a more aggressive, let-it-all-hang-out technique, should parallel the image of the company itself.

But keep in mind that the momentum of a company is so slow and ponderous that even if their stated goal is to change their image and direction they will still buy according to the old one. I recently had a series of meetings with Proctor & Gamble, who, fearing they are losing touch with the times, are desperately trying to modernize their consumer approach. It became apparent to me, however, that as much as they would like to, they are still bound to their old ways of looking at things, and it will take them a while to alter this course.

We recently approached Tiffany's regarding our desire to represent the licensing of their name. Two separate but related facts helped us bracket our approach.

First, Tiffany's had recently been bought by Avon, a publicly held, bottom-line company, which implied to me that Tiffany's would be more open to commercialization than they had been as a privately held, elitist one. Second, Tiffany's was still Tiffany's, and part of its attractiveness to

Avon as an acquisition certainly had to be in the implicit quality of the name. If "licensing" conjured up images of Smurfs or Cabbage Patch dolls, we wouldn't get to first base. Our best approach was similar to the one we had taken with Wimbledon, which was to stress visibility and quality—how licensing, if undertaken with selectivity, discrimination, and taste, would serve to enhance the up-market value of the Tiffany name

Getting to the Right Guy

One of the biggest problems we have had as a sales organization is figuring out who within another company will be making a decision on what. Very often in our business we don't know if it's the advertising department, the marketing department, or someone in PR or corporate communications. It may very well turn out to be the chairman and CEO of a multibillion-dollar corporation if the subject is of personal interest to him.

In certain companies, particularly multinational, multi-segmented operations, it is almost impossible to figure out the decision-making process, or to find any sort of central authority. Decisions seem to be made by some mysterious consensus that even the highest echelons of management can't explain. This, of course, is a problem in dealing with companies of this sort, and very often the only solution is not to deal with them at all.

In most companies, however, the decision-making process is not only there somewhere, it is discernible—as are the names of the decision makers. To find them, it is mostly a matter of doing your homework and asking the right questions.

If You Don't Know, Ask

Most sales are not cold calls. There is some contact or connection which gets you thinking about a particular company in the first place.

Most people are only too happy to tell you everything you need to know about the company they work for, such as how it is structured and who reports to whom. Without much coaxing (and by knowing when to remain silent) you can learn almost anything else you want to know—the company's priorities, its problems, its strengths and weaknesses, internal squabbles, power struggles, and so on. This kind of information is useful because a company's real decision-making process is rarely the way it looks on a flow chart.

Of course, you have to consider the source of the information and filter it through your reading of that person. People will often imply that you should be dealing with them, but you can tell by the way they talk about someone else—in a jealous manner or in a way that contradicts what you already know—that the person they are describing is actually the person you need to see.

Another excellent source of information is anyone who has successfully dealt with that company before and therefore has some insight into its bureaucratic secrets. This can be their advertising agency, a friendly competitor, or even someone else within your own company.

Don't Be Misled by Titles

Assume almost nothing from titles. I used to think, for example, that the head of General Motors International would be an important decision maker in terms of GM's overseas operations. I soon found out that he had literally no decision-making authority, except in the broadest sense, and that GM companies throughout the world were almost totally autonomous.

The reasons why someone is called vice-president are as numerous as the vice-presidents. Even in companies where titles are justly awarded, there is always a lag time: people about to move up, people about to move down, and people about to move out. An assistant marketing manager may be the real marketing decision maker. There are also pet projects and oddball areas of authority that don't conform to any job description.

When David Foster, a golf lover, was chairman of Colgate, we knew that he would make every decision relating to their golf sponsorship, even down to where to place the latrines on the course. On the other hand, when I flew to Japan to discuss sponsorship of the women's pro tennis tour with Toyota, I discovered my meeting was with an "assistant manager" in the PR department. I began explaining how the sponsorship worked—this much for this, another half-million for the bonus pool, and so on—and the assistant manager kept nodding his head in agreement. I was sure I was talking to the wrong person and that this one didn't understand a word I was saying. We later got a signed contract for over $5 million.

Find a Star

And make him a friend. People both inside and outside our company are always telling me how "lucky" I am to have personal relationships with the CEOs of so many companies around the world. In the vast majority of these cases I had met these people, spotted their star quality, and made a concerted effort to get to know them many years before they became their company's chief executive officer, and in several cases before they had even entered the ranks of upper management.

One of the most important things anyone can do in

business is consider his or her future connections. Your contemporaries today will be running companies tomorrow. Find the stars in other companies and make them friends. Ten years from now—whether you're selling to them, buying from them, hiring them, or being hired by them—they will become one of your most important business assets.

The Multinational Rule

Remember, no top executive is ever happy with his company's international operations. Doing something for his company internationally will open the door for domestic opportunities as well.

Positioning

The word *positioning* in business has scores of meanings. A company "positions" itself for the future; a product is "positioned" for the marketplace; you "position" yourself for advancement or for a sale.

The word has so many business meanings, in fact, it can become meaningless. I am, therefore, defining it here very narrowly as it relates to your product or service.

In this sense, positioning is a matter of determining what someone is *really* buying when they buy your product or service and then *conveying* those impressions and motivations to the buyer.

This often requires converting human emotions into product characteristics: "Be a winner by going with a winner." It demands intelligence, savvy, and forethought and at its highest level becomes an art form with a tangible payoff: Your product or service is practically presold.

Positioning 1: Is It a Ford or a Mercedes?

Positioning is first and foremost a numbers game, going from mass—a Ford or Sears (affordability)—at one end of the market spectrum to elite—a Mercedes or Neiman-Marcus (quality, luxury)—at the other.

While elitism can be a potent buyer motivation, it can also be dangerous. Companies go just as broke positioning themselves above their market as below it.

A company must figure out where it fits in this spectrum— where the biggest bulge of its buyers is.

We recently finalized a fascinating licensing/endorsement/spokesperson deal for Arnold Palmer with Sears (similar in concept to Sears's arrangement with Cheryl Tiegs). It was fascinating to me because of its irony.

For two decades we had consciously positioned Arnold at the upper end of the market spectrum, affiliating him with such brands and companies as Rolex, Cadillac, Robert Bruce, and Hertz. Sears, meanwhile, had recently concluded that rising buyer sophistication had pushed them down a couple of notches from where they wanted to be. When Sears decided to upgrade its image, Arnold, like Cheryl, was an ideal choice. Had it not been for Arnold's previous "upmarket" affiliations, he would not have been so perfect.

Positioning 2: Weighing the Facts

A good salesman can take ten facts about a product and by stressing some and deemphasizing others create ten different impressions. That's what salesmanship really is: positioning the facts to get the desired response.

The incredible success in Japan of the American golfer Laura Baugh was a direct result of how we chose to position the facts.

Laura was an all-American type—cute, blond, vivacious—

who had shown great promise as a California amateur. But at seventeen years old she had yet to prove herself on the pro tour.

We knew the Japanese liked all-American types almost as much as they liked golf. But since Laura could not be marketed as a champion, we chose to play down her golfing prowess altogether. Instead, we positioned her as a kind of American beauty queen who happened to play a great game of golf.

The results were extraordinary—posters, calendars, endorsements, an endless stream of licensing opportunities. She became the hottest attraction in Japan, even hosting her own prime-time television show. By the time she returned to the United States to join the pro tour, her positioning was already well established.

Laura has yet to win a professional golf tournament, but she has probably earned more money off the course than any player in the history of women's golf.

Another example is model Jean Shrimpton, who in the late 1960s and early 1970s was known as "the most famous face in the world."

When Jean retired from modeling, she moved to Cornwall, England, and embraced the role of wife and mother.

The striking contrast in lifestyles—from glamour, flash-bulbs, and *Vogue* covers to English country gentlewoman—provided an interesting positioning opportunity, that of a world-famous model giving up all the glamour for the simpler pleasures of family life. Now Jean has the opportunity to work just a few days a year for handsome fees doing "family-style" commercials for margarine and other household products.

Positioning 3: Doing It with Mirrors

This is the most sophisticated type of positioning, and it can go wrong as often as it goes right. It doesn't mean belying or ignoring the facts but reflecting them in such a way that it creates the desired perception. It is done by beginning with the perception and working backward.

The best example I can give of this is "The Killy Challenge," a network television show we created in the wake of Jean-Claude Killy's three Olympic gold medals.

It was important to Killy's ongoing merchandising credibility that he continue to be perceived as a "winner"—as the best in the world. "The Killy Challenge" was a series of downhill races in which world-class skiers would challenge Killy's supremacy. But since Killy was "the best," the challenger would always be given a handicap—a head start—and in skiing a handicap of several seconds can mean several hundred feet.

Visually, the drama was never a matter of Killy winning or losing but whether or not he would catch up after spotting another skier several hundred feet. It was Killy, "the best in the world," against *himself*, with the other skier serving as a measuring stick. The desired impression was achieved even before he left the starting gate.

Positioning 4: Imaging

Another type of positioning involves *transcending* the facts—associating your product or service with positive, desirable values which have little or nothing to do with the product itself.

This is an approach often taken by the blue chip companies: Coca-Cola has positioned itself right up there with mom and apple pie; AT&T and GE stress family values and "homey" feelings; the oil companies have become "environmentalists"; and IBM and Xerox promote their standard of excellence, positioning themselves above their competitors.

We do this on a lesser scale with our sports clients. Athletes don't go on winning forever, and we've always felt it was important to "get them off the playing field" as quickly as we could.

This doesn't mean forced retirement. It does mean positioning them in such a way that their fame is no longer dependent on winning championships or dominating the sport that made them famous in the first place.

For our golf and tennis clients, we usually avoid what we call the "win ads"—television or print advertising geared to the client's status as a current champion of a major tournament. After all, what happens when he or she is no longer the "current" champion? Calling Bjorn Borg the "five-time Wimbledon champion" totally overshadows the fact that he is no longer even playing at Wimbledon.

Jackie Stewart is another example: He has not raced competitively in a decade, yet his image as an automotive expert, a "connoisseur of aerodynamics," *transcends* his sport, his need to win—or even to race.

How to Determine Value

A lot of the time you can't. But the usual business answers— "what someone is willing to pay" or "what it costs us to make"—are often worse than no answer at all. Consumer product businesses are particularly guilty of this: Pricing becomes a function of manufacturing costs.

In determining the value of what you're selling, it's helpful to ask yourself some of these questions:

- How unique is it? Can they buy it for less from my competitor? If so, are there some real qualitative advantages to my product?
- Can I sell it for more to their competition?
- How badly or how quickly do they need it?
- What would it cost to replace it?
- Are there any precedents that can help me?

- Is there a "passion factor"? Suppose you get a craving to buy an ice cream cone and when you get to the shop you discover the price has doubled. Are you still going to buy it?
- Is this a one-time deal, or is this the future?

When you have a pretty good idea of value, don't be afraid to name your price. In fact, this is the negotiating instance when it may be to your advantage to go first.

When value is guesswork, try to protect yourself in other ways in the event of success:

A number of years ago, the Norfolk and Western Railroad was trying to get the Fuji Iron & Steel Company's rail business in the United States. They learned that Fuji's president was a golf fanatic, and a Jack Nicklaus fan in particular, and so they approached us about arranging a golf date between Fuji's president and Jack in Japan. We charged $10,000 (This was the mid-1960s!) plus expenses (We had to get Jack to Japan anyway) and felt pretty good about the deal.

Five years later I ran into the vice-president of Norfolk and Western. He brought up the Nicklaus–Fuji golf outing and said, "You know, we've done about $17 million of shipping with Fuji since then."

We couldn't have known that, but neither could Norfolk and Western. Since, I've often asked myself why I hadn't added "plus 1 percent of any business this generates." I think they would have said "Fine."

9 | Stratagems

Placing

PEOPLE OFTEN UNDERESTIMATE THE importance of a conducive sales atmosphere. Just as there is a right time to make a sale there is usually a right place for it as well. The worst place may be the buyer's office. It can't compare to over lunch, after a tennis game, on a golf course, or anyplace where his receptivity is likely to be up and his guard is likely to be down.

I know of a producer who received a commitment for sixty-five hours of family television programming on the basis of a half-hour pilot. He screened the pilot on a Saturday at the television executive's home, in his den, on his giant TV screen, with the executive's wife and two kids—while they all ate popcorn. What could the executive say: "I don't like it. Give me back my popcorn and get out of my house"?

One of our most effective services is directed towards helping our corporate clients "place" their sales effort. We arrange, for instance, annual ski outings for *Time Magazine* and annual golf outings for *Newsweek* for the purpose of entertaining the CEO's of their key advertisers. The settings are invariably spectacular, and if you are a skiier or golfer, where would you rather talk business—in your office, or at a ski lodge in Sun Valley or at the clubhouse at St. Andrews? (It also gives these magazines a direct link to the top if anything goes wrong at the ad level).

A chance encounter at a non-business locale can also present an opportunity. Have you ever unexpectedly run into a strictly business associate at a beach or tennis club? Some awkwardness usually accompanies the experience because both parties want to avoid "talking business" like the plague. Bring it up anyway. Not only will it diffuse the awkwardness, it can set certain wheels in motion that can be followed up back at the office.

The Preconditions of a Sale

Over a period of several years, we had tried to sell Ford and its Lincoln Mercury division all sorts of projects that our company was involved in. I literally deluged Ben Bidwell, then general manager of Lincoln Mercury, with proposal after proposal. One day, probably out of a sense of frustration, he called me and said, "Mark, you really have no idea how to sell the Ford Motor Company, and if you would bring a couple of your people up here and let us explain to you, it would save us both a lot of time in the future."

I took two of our executives up to Dearborn, Michigan, where over the course of several hours we received a thorough indoctrination into what Ford was looking for, how we should present it, and whom we should be presenting it to.

That meeting led to the creation of the World Invitational Tennis Classic, which was enthusiastically sponsored by Ford and televised over the ABC network for the next several years.

But even more important, I came away with an understanding of the two preconditions of almost any successful sales effort:

First find out what they want to buy. If you don't know, ask, and let them tell you. Find out a company's problems, then show them how "we can work together" to solve them. It is so much easier to sell someone what they want to buy than it is to convince them to buy what you are selling.

Second, find out who does the buying. Every company has its system, procedures, and pecking order for making decisions. Don't always buck it.

Get Some No's

People have a need to say no. So let them.

If you have a shopping list, throw in a few ringers. Collect some negative currency before you get to whatever it is you really want to sell.

If you're only there to sell one thing, make a suggestion or assumption and let them tell you you're wrong. People also have a need to feel smarter than you are.

A few well-placed "no's" create the right environment for a "yes."

Sell Defensively

The Hertzes and the Avises, the Cokes and the Pepsis are not the only companies in the world looking over their shoulder and reacting strongly to their competition. I would say that 99.999 percent of companies do.

So find out whom your would-be clients hate. That knowledge can help you push them toward your deal, particularly if they are sitting on the fence ready to teeter off to one side or the other.

Expose Rather than Sell

Many times our best sales approach has been merely to expose a product to a prospective buyer and let the exposure speak for itself. The buyer's mind runs rampant with possibilities, and in his own words he begins to tell you—and to convince himself in the process—what it is that he wants to buy.

This technique has been particularly effective for us in selling commercial tie-ins to special events such as the Nobel Prize awards and the Wimbledon championships. Merely exposing a customer to the tradition and prestige of these events—as guests of the king and queen of Sweden or of the All-England Club—is the only selling that is really needed. They soak up the atmosphere and become enveloped in it, and from that moment on they want to be part of the experience, will begin to develop their own promotional "fits," and will start to sell us.

If you have confidence in your product and know the customer will ultimately be satisfied, an equally effective variation is to expose him to it by giving it away. In our effort to convince companies to make promotional use of our golfers or tennis players, we have often provided the client at no compensation, knowing that the client's personality and personability would help us do the convincing.

I am also a great believer in offering a product or service and telling the customer that we can establish the price later on, or that he can establish it for us, based on what he felt it was worth. Again, you have to know your customer. There are people we deal with who would just as soon add another zero and there are those who are more likely to subtract one.

Get Them a Little Bit Pregnant

When a company expresses genuine interest in your idea, product, or concept, start to get them a little bit pregnant.

Collect—aggressively solicit—their opinions on the deal and allow these to shape your idea or presentation: "We were wondering such-and-such"; "Would it be better to emphasize this or that?"; "We'd like to know your feelings on the following."

It is better to solicit this kind of information in a letter, which requires more thought to answer. For the same reason it is also better to avoid questions that can be answered yes or no.

There is nothing easier than selling someone his or her "own" idea, which is what this becomes.

If you can get enough answers on the details, people will commit themselves to the larger deal long before they are actually aware of it.

Similarly, you should determine mutually agreeable objectives beforehand which can be precisely defined and clearly stated. Any proposal, concept, or idea which directly responds to those objectives is halfway to being sold.

Use "Them"

The head of our television department approached me recently and asked me to attend a meeting. He anticipated closing a sale, but it was a complicated situation involving several parties. Everyone wanted to do the deal, but it had yet to be determined precisely how these parties would interact, that is, who would be doing what for how much. He felt my presence would be helpful to "our side."

I felt the opposite and chose not to attend. My reasoning was very similar to my feelings about handling a crisis: The best first reaction is no reaction at all. My presence would have meant that I would have to react. I wanted to keep our options open until we had a chance to analyze the results of this meeting. I preferred that this executive have to check back with "them" (meaning, in this case, me), before making any final commitments.

People use the absent, undefined "them" all the time in selling, but I think it is usually done as a matter of practicality rather than calculation. In most cases people really do have to check with someone else. "They" or "them" is just as useful in those cases where they don't.

Outside our company, most people I deal with assume that I am the final decision-making authority, but I will rarely commit myself until I have "consulted" with the appropriate executive or division head.

The converse of this can also work to your advantage. In any new business situation, when someone tells me "I'm the decision maker around here" and I have reason to believe this is true, my lips start to smack. He has already cut off his first line of defense.

Show Up

I first met the gentleman who heads our apparel division over twenty years ago. He was president of a major clothing manufacturing firm at the time, and he had called me in Cleveland to express an interest in affiliating Gary Player with one of his apparel lines. We decided we should meet and we did—at his office in New York at 9 AM the next morning.

Years later, he told me that when I offered him a job with our company this was one of the main reasons he had taken it. He had been so impressed by my hopping on a plane and showing up the next morning, he thought we would be an interesting company to work for.

Today my itinerary is so tight (and sometimes planned out six months in advance) that I can't do this as much as I'd like to. But one of the best sales techniques that I know of is to ask when can we meet and how soon—and then show up. Usually the farther you have to fly, the more impressive it is.

Divide and Conquer

This is probably more appropriately phrased "Unite and Conquer," though the people you are "uniting" may not always agree.

Suggest the same idea to two different key executives in the same company. If you can get them to agree separately that the idea is sound then, when you put them together, a sale is probably going to be the result.

What you are doing, in essence, is acting as their middleman. ("Bob, Bill really likes this." "Bill, Bob really likes this.") Each will be reassured by the other's desire to do the deal; each will be able to take credit for the concept; and each will feel less at risk. You will also be hastening the process of commitment by forcing a decision without seeming to do so.

We had a version of this used effectively on us, which we began referring to internally as "the Fila trick."

Fila is the Italian sportswear company which manufactures and licenses Bjorn Borg's tennis wear. In the early days of Fila's development, their people would ask the same question—usually concerning what Borg would or would not do in terms of time commitments—of five or six people within our company. Since they were dealing with us in so many parts of the world, they became very proficient at this tactic. They would use what they were told in Australia to their best advantage in Japan; they would use what they were told in Japan to their best advantage in

England, and so on until they circled the globe—combining the best of each answer into one unbelievably favorable response.

Sell One to One

I hate sales presentations made to a large group of people and will avoid these situations whenever I can. To me, a large group is more than one.

Find the key guy and sell one to one. If you try to sell to more than one person at the same time, you are introducing into the sale the dynamics of *their* interrelationships, which can do nothing but detract from your purpose. You can't know who is there to impress whom, who is only interested in looking good, or in making someone else look bad. You may suspect, but unless you are working within their company you can't know.

Sell directly to the key person, and if he likes what you're proposing, he will know best how to sell it in.

The Chinese Menu Syndrome

There is usually more than one way to solve a marketing problem, and it is the seller's responsibility to find the best way and to emphasize that while deemphasizing the others. Don't get caught in the choose-one-from-column-A-and-two-from-column-B trap.

If you give the buyer a choice, you are introducing a whole new layer into the decision-making process. Not only are you asking a customer to make a commitment, you are also asking him, "Which one do you want to commit to?"

We have had situations where we proposed more than

one solution to a potential customer's problem. Frequently the result is that he will like something about each solution. That sounds terrific, but it isn't. By offering a choice, you often help the customer focus as well on what he doesn't like about each solution.

Remind Them of Your Glorious Past

I bring up Arnold Palmer's name in business conversations all the time, including those which have nothing to do with Arnold and, indeed, nothing to do with golf. It is simply that Arnold's financial success, and the role we played in it, are two of the things our company is best known for. As an individual, my relationship with Arnold is more often recognized than I am: "Oh, yeah. The guy who manages Arnold Palmer."

People in business want to do business with winners. It helps to make your present customers aware of either your own or your company's big wins in the past. Out-and-out bragging is not a very good idea, but it can be done subtly in a million other ways.

Bring in your credits and achievements, or your other blue chip clients, not as direct statements but as examples of the kinds of things you have done for others that you would like to do for them now.

Correspondence Tools

The format of standard business correspondence, when used with care and discretion, can be an interesting sales tool.

Open Copies to the Boss

This virtually assures you of a response, and probably a quicker one than you would get otherwise. Even if you don't know the superior, it will give the impression that you do.

Letters can also be written in such a way—though this technique is usually more advisable over the telephone—as to imply that the superior would really like to see the deal go through.

The pitfalls to open-copying a man's boss are obvious, particularly if you know the recipient will be the ultimate decision maker. Generally I use this as a last resort—once more traditional efforts have been exhausted and I am reasonably sure that the recipient, left to his own devices, will continue to ignore letters and phone calls.

Blind Copies to the Boss

A blind copy to the recipient's immediate superior can be even more effective. Of course, in this case you better know the superior and know that he will discuss the contents of your letter with the recipient.

This is most useful in those situations where your initial contact or discussions were with the superior and the subject of them has since been delegated to the recipient. It is therefore perfectly legitimate to copy the recipient's boss. Since it is a blind copy, the recipient, from that day forward, will never know who else you might be copying and is more likely to consider carefully the contents of your letter.

"Dictated but Not Read"

The legitimate use of this term, of course, is when you are unable to review a dictated letter once it has been typed. But it is also useful for sending up a trial balloon or phrasing something in a more aggressive way than you would have, had you had the "opportunity" to soften it.

If the recipient finds it offensive or overreacts to it, you have still made your point but can retract the way in which it was made.

Not Invented Here

The not-invented-here complex, or the trashing of an idea or concept by someone because he or she didn't originate it, is one of the biggest sales problems we have had to face in every division of our organization.

We are often contacted directly by companies inquiring about the services of one of our athletes or the implementation of a sports promotion. Once we have developed a program that everyone seems to like, the company feels compelled to run it by its advertising agency. The agency, because it did not originate the idea, feels equally compelled to punch holes in it.

I used to believe that the not-invented-here complex was unique to the nature of our business. But I have talked to enough people in enough different businesses now to understand that not only is the problem pervasive, it may be endemic. There's a tendency, maybe even a need, to knock any idea that isn't your own.

The conventional wisdom in dealing with this problem is "make them think it's their idea." This is perfectly good advice in selling but totally impractical and useless in dealing with not-invented-here. Any effort along these lines is going to seem transparent and patronizing.

The practical solution is to *make them see their self-interest.*

It is perfectly apparent to me, for instance, that if a proposal reaches the state of ad agency review, it means that someone (and more likely several someones) within the agency's client company already likes it. But I've seen paranoia become so rampant that the ad agency will start to tear apart the idea even before asking politically sensitive questions, such as who within the client company likes what and why.

Obviously if this is so apparent to me, it is my job to make it equally apparent to the person doing the reviewing—to show him where his self-interest probably lies.

Recently I met the chairman of a Fortune 500 company under quasi-business circumstances and during the course of a conversation with him mentioned a concept we were developing that I felt might be appropriate for his company. I could see his eyes light up, but he said that anything of this sort would have to originate with his promotion department and gave me the name of a particular person I should contact.

When I followed up several weeks later, the idea was met with overwhelming disinterest. I then related precisely the circumstances under which I had met the boss and the reaction I felt I had observed and suggested that it was in the promotion director's best interest to learn more about what we had in mind.

Ultimately, everybody won. We sold them the idea, it worked, and though the idea didn't originate with this particular person, he received sole credit within his company for its success.

Visual Aids

RockResorts, the Rockefeller family–owned chain of luxury resorts, was in the process of constructing one of the most glamorous resorts in Hawaii, called the Mauna Kea, and Laurance Rockefeller and his staff had flown out from New York for a full day of meetings. Crucial decisions had to be made involving millions of dollars in expenditures and commitments.

Apparently, fairly early on in these meetings someone brought out color swatches of the various motifs that were being considered for the table linens in the dining room. People in the room became so interested in the color swatches—each throwing in his decorating opinion—that when it came time for Rockefeller to fly back to New York most of the major issues were still unresolved.

I've never seen a bad idea sold because of great visual aids, and I've never seen a good idea go unsold because of lack of visual aids. Moreover, if not properly used and appropriately timed, visual aids (anything from charts and graphs to elaborate multimedia shows) can work against you.

First, people have opinions on everything. If you're not careful you can find the conversation deflected toward a critique of your visual aids rather than holding to what you are there to sell in the first place.

Second, if introduced too early in the presentation it can be distracting. All of a sudden everyone's playing with your visual aids while your sales strategy and game plan go out the window.

Until you are ready to get to the "show" part of the show and tell, keep your visual aids *out of sight*. You don't want people waiting and wondering what you've got in that little black box.

10|Negotiating

I HAVE HEARD OR READ on more than several occasions that I am a "tough" or a "hard-nosed" negotiator. It's probably not a bad reputation to have precede me—people expect me to ask big numbers—but I prefer to think of myself as an *effective* negotiator rather than a tough one.

I actually take more pride in my sales ability than in my negotiating skills, because it is much harder to make someone *want* to buy than it is to define the terms under which they are buying.

In fact, I often see negotiation as the last step in an ongoing sales effort, the culmination of a process that may have lasted several months or more.

When the time comes to negotiate, certain principles do apply.

What, When, Where, How Exclusive, and How Much?

All five of the questions asked above should be answered during the course of negotiation. Each can be expanded, limited, or traded off as the negotiation dictates.

Even in cases such as real estate where all five would not generally apply, it is still a useful list to run through. It might provide solutions ("Rather than buy this property from you, suppose I were to lease it for ninety-nine years") which weren't contemplated when the negotiation began.

The What

What is it, precisely, that you are selling? With celebrities it always comes down to two things: their name and their time. But this still leaves the "what" question far from answered. What rights are you selling to the name and time and for what use is it intended?

The When

This means how long, from "one contiguous eight-hour period," which can be used to define a work day, to "forever."

The Where

"Territory," which can range from "the world" to "south Cincinnati," is an interesting area for trade-offs and multinational, multiregional contracts. We have several television properties, for instance, which are licensed in more than a hundred territories, some of which are defined by national borders, others by a common language. It is because of the territorial aspect of negotiation that we maintain so many offices around the world—and thereby stay so many jumps ahead of our competitors.

The How Exclusive

We have found this to be an attractive negotiating chip. To what degree does the buyer wish (and are we willing) to shut out the rest of the competition? This can mean product exclusivity, industrywide exclusivity, territorial exclusivity, a "head start" exclusivity—all sorts of interesting things when linked to other aspects of the negotiation.

The How Much

This means money, but not necessarily money alone. It can also mean stocks, securities, or other forms of equity. For us, it often means "how much time." Time is an active professional athlete's most cherished commodity. He or she must spend a certain amount of time practicing or playing in tournaments or games. Since time can't be manufactured or expanded, we guard with a bulldog's tenacity the number of "personal days" an athlete must commit to a client.

Don't Get Hung Up on "How Much"

This always reminds me of the "baseball bat method" of choosing sides: About halfway up the handle you suddenly know how it's going to come out.

When one party starts out at twenty and the other party starts at ten and you end up with fifteen, that's not a negotiation; that's splitting the difference. Moreover, you run the risk of neither party being "happy" with fifteen and both feeling they are "losing" if they accept anything less.

Don't deal with numbers in isolation. Negotiation is more

intricate and subtle than that. Numbers are just one piece—no bigger and no smaller than the other pieces—of the negotiating pie.

Big Companies Don't Mean Big Bucks

The bigger the company, the more money they have to spend.

In theory this is true; in practice it is quite the opposite. The bigger the company, the more compartmentalized they are, which means the more budgets that need to be tapped in order to come up with the necessary financing.

I've seen multimillion-dollar commitments made by one person in a medium-sized company, and I've seen one of the biggest companies in America require six different decisions by six different divisions to approve a $50,000 expenditure.

Let the Other Guy Go First

Very often, it's a good idea to let the other party take first crack at the terms and numbers. At the very least it tells you something about what he's thinking. And there have been many occasions when the other party's first offer was higher than the opening or even the closing figure I had in mind.

Sometimes you can pull out the numbers from the other party by asking a series of hypothetical questions based primarily on the other terms: "If you were to do this and we were to do that, how much could that be worth?" "Suppose we were to throw in this and add that?" "Suppose you were to put a dollar figure on it?"

Play in the Majors

When confronted with naming your terms or price, counter by recalling a similar deal which establishes your "ball park," albeit the best possible ball park you wish to be in: "When we recently sold 'X' to company 'Y,' we received '$Z.' "

There is no implicit challenge in this approach. It gets your point across without moving the other party into a defensive position . . . and it gets him thinking at higher levels.

Don't Deal in Round Numbers

Round numbers beg to be negotiated, usually by counter-offer round numbers. Odd numbers sound harder, firmer, less negotiable.

I hate to hear "a hundred thousand dollars" as a number thrown out in negotiations. That's the world's most negotiable number. Make it $95,500 or $104,500. Either way you're probably going to end up with more.

Deal in Psychological Currencies

Over the years we have made great use of psychological negotiating chips—deal points which seem innocent enough on the surface but carry with them potent underlying psychological impact. They make excellent negotiating currency because their power is rarely understood by the other party. I can recall countless occasions when we have used this to break deadlocks—to give the other parties exactly what they wanted while keeping them totally unaware of how much more we were getting in return.

One of my earliest examples of this occurred during our negotiation with Slazenger/Australia over the length of Gary Player's equipment contract. Slazenger wanted a short-term contract: one year with renewable options. We were loath to give it because if for some reason it did not work out Gary would then be "damaged goods" as far as his equipment affiliation in Australia was concerned. But Slazenger would not budge an inch—or, in this case, a day—which is when we came up with what we later began to refer to internally as our "Australian termination clause": The contract was made terminable by either party from the moment it was signed—but on five years' notice.

My theory was that Slazenger would be reluctant to terminate anyone whom they would still be affiliated with personally and committed to financially for another five years and would work harder to see that this never happened.

Gary's contract with Slazenger is presently in its twentieth year.

In the late 1960s we reached a similar impasse with Allstate Life Insurance and Arnold Palmer, again involving the length of the contract. We wanted a fifteen-year contract, and while Judson Branch, CEO of Allstate at the time, did not object, he was planning to retire soon and did not want to burden his successor with a long-term contract. He was therefore insisting on a three-year contract with options to renew.

This concerned me even more than it normally would because I knew who the new CEO was going to be, knew that his ego could not stand sharing the spotlight with Arnold, and knew he would probably never extend or renew the contract if he could get out of it cleanly.

What we ultimately agreed upon was a fifteen-year contract terminable after three years with the payment of a penalty fee. The key was to make the penalty fee slightly larger than the annual retainer fee.

I had two theories on this one. First, it is one thing not to renew a contract and psychologically quite another to have to go to Arnold and say, "We want to terminate you." Second, even if Allstate did decide to terminate, I felt I could convince them to extend for an additional year (and then another and then another) as long as the termination penalty was larger than the annual retainer.

The contract continued on for many years even under the new CEO.

Avoid Showdowns

Somehow, negotiating has become confused with machismo, as though the whole point is to outlast your opponent, to make him back down first.

The point of negotiation is to reach an agreement that is mutually advantageous to both parties. To make it a contest of egos can only work against you. Don't use phrases like "deal breaker," "take it or leave it," or "that's nonnegotiable" —anything that makes you sound like you're daring the other person to knock a chip off your shoulder.

Don't raise controversial issues which have only an indirect or insignificant relationship to the deal being discussed or to the ongoing relationship.

These issues, too, are often the result of ego or a kind of bravado: "Then you can't do this" or "Then we're going to exclude that." In many cases these issues have a way of turning into deal points which you would otherwise win by fiat.

Negotiate Backward

I find it helpful to try to figure out in advance where the other person would like to end up—at what point he will do the deal and still feel like he's coming away with something.

This is different from "How far will he go?" A lot of times you can push someone to the wall and you'll still reach an agreement, but his resentment will come back to haunt you in a million ways.

The best way to find out the "magic point" of a negotiation is to ask—if somewhat indirectly.

We try to get a sales estimate: "By affiliating so-and-so with your product, how many units do you anticipate selling?"

Usually they'll inflate the figure a little bit to impress you with their expertise. But we can use that figure to determine a dollar guarantee that they can live with, and we can back it up with *their* logic.

Trade Places

Another way to find the magic point is to put yourself in the other guy's shoes. Run through a series of questions and answer them *as if you were he*: "What are 'my' real limitations?" "How badly do 'I' want this deal to happen?" "What are 'my' options if it falls through?" "Will 'I' look good, or will 'I' have to always be defending this internally?" "And what trade-offs can 'I' get to assure that this doesn't happen?"

This can often help you envision where you are going to end up with amazing clarity.

Mollify Then Modify: The Use of "But" and "However"

Acknowledge the other party's feelings. This is the oldest psychological technique in the world and works just as well in negotiations as it does in any other form of human relations. It sounds as though you have accepted or committed to something, when in truth all you have "accepted" is how the other party feels.

The conjunctive clause, which allows you to cancel out the first part of a sentence, is a wonderful negotiating tool: "Yes, but . . ."; "I know how you feel, but . . ."; "I know exactly what you mean and I couldn't agree with you more, but . . ."

People who have mastered this technique can get blood out of a stone. They have a way of turning almost any negotiation into a penitent–confessor relationship.

Deflect With a Question

If you don't like what you're hearing, respond with a question, even if it's no more than "Why are you saying that?" It may cause the other side to scrutinize their position a little more closely. It softens your response. At the very least it keeps them talking while you keep listening.

Question Positions but Don't Ignore Them

I have been in many negotiations where I have said something or responded in some way and the other person has continued talking as though I had never opened my mouth.

There is nothing more frustrating in any sort of business communication, or more disruptive to negotiation, than to get the feeling you are talking to someone with a hearing defect.

Playing dumb is a valid negotiating technique, and "I don't understand" is a legitimate negotiating response. But to ignore the other party's position or to pretend you didn't even hear it because you didn't want to hear it will only build up frustrations. Moreover, the more the other party is forced to repeat his or her position, the more that position is going to harden.

Sweeten with His Self-Interest

Another negotiating technique that I have found effective is to sweeten the deal with things that aren't that important to me but could be important to him. This can include terms which have little or nothing to do with the deal at hand.

We have, for instance, agreed to provide particularly hard-to-get seats to the Olympics in a contract that otherwise has nothing to do with the Olympics. On another occasion a social golf outing was arranged between one of our golf clients and the boss of the person we were negotiating with.

The absolute masters of this technique are members of both houses of Congress who, as a matter of course, coattail the interests of their constituents—and thereby their own—onto bills that have absolutely nothing to do with their local dam projects or fish hatcheries.

Never overlook the barter possibilities of throwing in quantities of your product, which you get at cost but which are valued by the other party at something closer to retail.

Keep Your Time Frame to Yourself

The pressure to get a deal done can make you say and do things that aren't in your best interest. Whether your deadline is real and absolute (it rarely is), or merely desirable or convenient, don't let the other party know about it. If the other party knows you have a deadline, they really don't need to know—or give on—anything else.

Conversely, their deadline is one of the most valuable pieces of information you can extract from them.

Time itself—or the passing of it—can also be one of your most valuable negotiating allies. Anxiety and the desire to get a deal done breed hyperkinetic behavior. There is a natural tendency to speed up the negotiation process rather than to slow it down. Force yourself to resist this urge, and take advantage of it in others.

In any negotiation which is drawing to a close but in which issues remain to be resolved, I have conditioned myself over the years to request automatically that it be carried over to the next day. This, at the very least, gives me time to clear my head and often results in the other party making major concessions just so he doesn't have to spend another night thinking about it.

It is also worth remembering that agreement isn't needed on every point in order to reach a deal. We have a significant percentage of contracts in our files which stipulate that certain points will be resolved in the future so as to let the basic agreement proceed.

Using Emotion

Negotiations are seldom formal, sit-around-the-table affairs. In fact, almost any form of business problem or disagreement—from a threatened union walkout to "Who's going to pay this $500 expense?"—is resolved by some form of negotiation. The less formal these negotiations are, the more likely emotion is going to play some part. Whoever controls the emotional content of these disputes is almost always going to walk away with the bigger winning.

Perceive any Business Dispute as the Beginning of a Negotiation

Simply by perceiving it this way, you will become more calculating and less likely to respond in your own worst interest. Psychologically, your focus will be more on getting what you want and less on getting something off your chest.

Step Back and Relax

Counter emotional outbursts by going emotionally limp. Say anything except what you probably want to say. "Let me think about that," or "I'll call you back." Perceive it as a game with winners and losers because that's what it is: a game of wits—and who's going to be the first to lose theirs.

See Emotional Outbursts as Opportunities

This is negotiation through counterpunching. Once the other party has thrown the first emotional blow, he has given up a certain amount of control. Depending on how you respond you can accept that control or give it right back to him.

WHAT THEY DON'T TEACH YOU AT HARVARD BUSINESS SCHOOL

Act in Anger but Never React in Anger

Anger, and other strong emotions, can be effective negotiating tools, but only as a calculated act, never as a reaction. I read somewhere that a photo of Nikita Khrushchev's historic shoe-pounding incident at the UN revealed that he was still wearing both his shoes. A third "for-pounding-only" shoe? That's calculation.

Get Them Charged Up about Side Issues

Effective negotiating demands an absolute clarity of purpose, an ability to keep mentally focused on the ends while all the while discussing the means. If you suspect someone is not a very good negotiator—even though he prides himself on being one—he will almost always be satisfied with a few side victories if you make them seem to be more than that. Get him charged up about side issues, make "reluctant" concessions, and then walk home with the big prize.

Use Candor

Candor, when properly used, is one of the most powerful, effective—and underused—negotiating techniques I know of. When negotiations become excessively tense, are about to get out of hand, or are in danger of falling through, a moment of candor—"Look, I really want this to go through" or "This is very important to me"—not only brings back perspective, it often totally disarms the other party.

An impasse which moments earlier seemed insurmountable will start to disintegrate. And a conciliation, which moments before seemed unthinkable, will seem possible after all.

Are You Negotiating from Strength or Weakness?

This is an important question to ask yourself before actual negotiations begin and can usually be answered from the selling effort alone. How hard can you push? How badly does the other party want this deal to happen? How does the other party perceive your position?

There is a vast difference, of course, between legitimate positions of strength and weakness and the *perception* of those positions. The game aspect of negotiation is saying and doing things which puncture those perceptions that come too close to reality while encouraging those perceptions which are furthest from the truth. Internally, we call this "swooping and darting," or not letting the other party get a fix on our position.

If you are negotiating from strength, the more you let your strength be known, the more the other party will go out of his way to disabuse you of it. Even the most obvious compromises will become concession standoffs, with the other party insisting on winning all the minor points because he knows he will have to fold on the big ones.

The other danger of negotiating from strength is that there is a tendency just to get the deal done rather than to get the best deal. Strength in a negotiation seems to quell one's desire to hang tough—to fight for all the minor points because the bigger ones have already been conceded. Yet it is these fringe areas that make the difference between a good agreement and a so-so one.

The final point in negotiating is to get as much as you can but to *get something*. Over the years I have run into many people who consider themselves excellent tough negotiators, and yet for every deal they rammed down someone's throat there were two that fell through.

Once two parties have acknowledged in some way that they can both benefit from agreement—which is usually the stage at which a negotiation begins—it is inexcusable, barring unforeseen circumstances, not to reach one.

Contracts

One party generally benefits more than the other from vague or nonbinding language in a contract or letter agreement. Determine up front whether a vague agreement or an airtight one better suits your purpose.

I prefer letter agreements to more formally constructed contracts. Blue-bound documents tend to scare people. A well-drafted contract is one that is airtight, contains almost no legal phraseology, and reads like a letter from home.

Always draft first. Once you begin the process of converting deal points into language, scores of questions come up. You want the opportunity to get your version down on paper first.

There is one exception to this. If you are in unfamiliar legal territory, it is often quite revealing to see what the other party considers important by what they have included in the contract.

When redraft language comes back, treat it in a covering or amendment letter rather than drafting again from scratch and forcing the entire contract to be re-reviewed. (It is impossible for a lawyer to go through a contract a second time without coming up with additional points.)

The "definitions" section of a contract should be care fully scrutinized if you are on the reviewing end and scoured for opportunity if you are doing the drafting. What something is legally called can alter everything else in the contract.

Many years ago, when we were negotiating Gary Player's golf club contract with Shakespeare Golf, we wished to have the right to do a separate deal for golf grips. Golf grips are sold to golfers who want their clubs regripped because they are old or have lost their feel, and while this was totally noncompetitive with the Shakespeare agreement, we knew if we raised this issue they would resist. And so in the "definitions" section of the contract we narrowly defined a "golf iron" as a "metal flange attached to a metal or fiberglass shaft by means of a hozzle." We made no mention of grips, ultimately did a separate deal with a grip company, and the Shakespeare–Player agreement continued amicably for many years.

Legal phraseology should be considered red flags. Lawyers can draw from a litany of words, terms, and phrases which are intended to reverse the meaning of everything that comes before or after.

Break down guarantees and royalties into their lowest common denominator. If the contract includes more than one product or more than one territory, divide the guarantees, get them allocated accordingly, and make each a separate account. (There have been many occasions—separately accounting Australia and England comes immediately to mind—where this has resulted in hundreds of thousands of dollars more in royalty income.)

Speed of execution is critical. Enthusiasm for a deal diminishes as time goes by.

Don't send contracts directly to legal departments but to the people with whom you are dealing. They are likely to be just as impatient with their own legal department as you are. Internally, they will often take your best position against their own legal department ("that's a meaningless point") just to get it out of legal.

III
Running a Business

11 | Building a Business

TODAY THE INTERNATIONAL MANAGEMENT
Group is a management, consulting, and marketing firm operating out of fifteen offices around
the world. The activities of its twelve companies range from
career management of many of the world's leading sports
personalities, to organizing and implementing sports events
throughout the world to operating fashion model agencies
in New York and London. This year, gross revenues will
exceed $200 million, which makes us a small to medium-
sized company in the general scheme of things but a major
force in the business of sports: We are involved in over
forty of them.

I did not envision what has come to pass when I first
shook hands with Arnold Palmer back in 1960. At the time,
I was a young lawyer simply looking for a way to combine
one of my lifelong passions—golf—with my day-to-day business activities. (This still may be one of the better ways to
start a business: What are you really passionate about in
life, and is there any way to make a living at it?)

As an amateur golfer I was good enough to qualify for the
1958 U.S. Open but smart enough to know I would never
make it big on the pro tour. For me the next best thing was
representing those who did.

In assessing the decisions we made that helped us grow,

I realize that there is nothing we have done that was all that unique or unconventional. The success we have had—and I'm immodest enough to think we've had quite a bit—is confirmation that the things that are supposed to work really do work and the things that aren't supposed to don't.

A lot of building a business is listening to your own common sense, then taking the necessary steps to turn the theories into practice.

Commit (Early on) to Quality

When I first started representing Arnold he had won one major championship in 1958, which was followed by a lackluster year in 1959. Our second client, Gary Player, was barely known at all in the United States when we signed him, though in the 1958 U.S. Open Gary finished second to Tommy Bolt and impressed me with his courage and his determination to play well in strange surroundings under extreme pressure. When we began representing our third client, Jack Nicklaus, he was still an amateur.

Arnold, Jack, and Gary are three totally different personality types, but all three possessed the quality—class—that would make them champions off the golf course as well as on it. They were not just first-rate golfers; they were first-rate people.

I was simply trying to sign up the best golfers I could who also seemed to have the kind of character a company would want to be associated with. I didn't realize until later—fortunately, not much later—that I was, in fact, making a "commitment to quality."

I can't think of any business where such a commitment doesn't apply. Start with the best, or what you think is going to be the best; it will get you started on the right foot. It's the only absolute competitive edge, and it's like working with a net: a hedge that will minimize bad decisions and maximize good ones in the future.

Be Smart Enough to Know When You're Lucky

As it turned out, Palmer, Player, and Nicklaus would totally dominate the world of golf for two decades. By 1969 they had won twenty of golf's major championships, and the list of Masters champions from 1960 to 1966 read like this: Palmer, Player, Palmer, Nicklaus, Palmer, Nicklaus, and Nicklaus.

They became known as the Big Three of golf, and if they had been 3 of our first 20 clients, or even 3 of our first 10, my whole philosophy about business might have been different. But with 250 golfers out on the tour, we had gone 3 for 3. It was like winning a lottery.

Lady Luck had been kind to us, as I think she often is to a lot of businesses. And while I'm sure we had helped make our luck, this initial success had been far too phenomenal simply to take it in stride, congratulate ourselves on how smart we were, and wait for lightning to strike again.

I think that was one of the most important decisions we ever made. We were going to accept our good fortune for what it was, but we weren't going to sit around until another "Big Three" came along.

Grow Slowly

Of the twenty-odd years we have been in business, the first six—or nearly a third of our life span—were limited to representing professional golfers. I felt we had too much to learn to do anything else. I also wanted to get better before we got bigger.

So many companies, particularly in this high tech age, are unwilling to do this. They would rather grow quickly than profit quickly. If these companies would slow down a little, take some time to analyze their success, and allow their depth of management to catch up, I think they would see that they could have both—a healthy growth rate and healthy profitability.

It's a simple business truth that you can't stay the same size. But we resisted, and continue to resist, the pressure to grow too fast.

By 1966 we had become a major presence in golf. We were organized, we had the right people in place, and we knew where we were going. I thought we had better diversify.

Diversify Your Expertise

If we have had a formula for growth it has been to start with the best, learn from the best, expand slowly and solidify our position, then horizontally diversify our expertise.

By the mid-1960s we had thought about expanding for some time, and the most obvious choices—tennis was still an amateur sport—were any of the three major team sports, football, baseball, or basketball. But we had learned a couple of things which made this choice less obvious.

First, we were not agents as much as managers. Agents are guys who book bands and negotiate player contracts with team owners. There were no team owners in golf.

Our interest and expertise had always been in developing income opportunities for our clients off the playing field, in establishing licensing and promotional relationships, and in managing them in a way that would provide those athletes with a steady income long after their playing days were over. I also felt the regionality of most team sports athletes would severely restrict their marketability. Golfers, on the other hand, were almost as salable in Tokyo or in Kalamazoo as they were in their home towns.

Second, I was pretty well convinced that the "weekend

warrior," the guy who played golf once or twice a week and watched sports on television, could more readily identify with Arnold Palmer, hitching up his pants on the eighteenth tee and then splitting the fairway with a 300-yard drive, than with anonymous people in pads and helmets.

Our goal, therefore, was to branch out into other individual sports, preferably those with an international profile, and sign individual stars who would benefit from our total management approach to representation. We signed Jackie Stewart, who was the world's leading race driver, in 1969, and soon added a score of other world-class drivers, including Peter Revson, Mark Donohue, Francois Cevert, and Graham Hill. (At the time we failed to recognize the major difference between golfers and auto racers: Golf doesn't kill you. The emotional price was high.)

In 1968, when tennis abandoned its amateur status, we were able to sign Rod Laver and Margaret Court, then the world's leading male and female players.

The year 1968 also produced another opportunity, the Olympics, and skiing's first international superstar, Jean-Claude Killy.

Each of these sports has since produced a stable of clients which has given us prominence—and dominance—in these areas.

We began diversifying our expertise in other ways. Representing golf's elite had given us the opportunity to learn quite a bit about a number of other businesses. We took advantage of this knowledge and established a separate golf equipment company for Arnold and two internal apparel divisions, one of which was later sold to NBC. In the late 1960s we also signed our first two nonsports clients, Hank Ketcham, the creator of Dennis the Menace, and Jean Shrimpton, the world-famous model.

Hire the Best to Teach You What You Don't Know

Today I believe in the importance of training more than the importance of hiring, which, after twenty years, may be an indication of our company's maturity. But when you're building a company, you sometimes hit gaps in knowledge which you know you'll have to fill if you want to continue to grow.

In the 1960s an unholy alliance was developing. Sports was helping to make television, and television was helping to make sports. Each was using the other to its own advantage, and so successfully it was (and still is) impossible to predict where it would all end. We weren't ignorant of television, but we felt our experience was limited enough to be dangerous.

About this time a vice-president at MCA by the name of Jay Michaels approached me on behalf of MCA's chairman, Lew Wasserman. Michaels was something of a legend in the television business. He had engineered the network deal for the fledgling American Football League, which gave the AFL its foothold and ultimately led to its merger with the NFL. Probably no one knew more about the incestuous relationship between sports and television.

Michaels told me that Wasserman was thinking about starting a leisure sports division and wanted to know if I was interested in running it for them.

After some soul searching and some discussions with several of our key executives and some of our top clients, I declined. I felt our independence was too important, and since we were still growing, I thought we might be stifled by being part of a larger, more established company.

But not too long after this I approached Jay Michaels. I told him of our desire to become more involved in the television business. I told him what I felt the potential was, the degree of commitment I was willing to make in order to realize that potential—and I told him I wanted his help.

I happened to hit him with the right situation at the right time, and in 1967 he came to work for us as the head of our newly formed television division, Trans World International.

Today TWI is the world's leading independent producer of sports programming and the world's largest representative of television rights to international sporting events. We produce or coproduce nearly 200 hours of sports programming each year, including "The Superstars" and "Battle of the Network Stars" for ABC, numerous skiing and track and field events for CBS, and "The World Professional Figure Skating Championships" and "The Chevrolet World Championships of Women's Golf" for NBC. We represent international television rights for, among others, Wimbledon, the U.S. Tennis Open, the National Football League, NCAA basketball, and most of the major golf championships.

TWI has also produced dozens of documentaries for such events as Wimbledon, the British Open, and the U.S. Open. It also represents a number of sportscasters, including John Madden, Jimmy "the Greek" Snyder, Chris Shienkel, and Al Michaels . . . Jay Michaels's son.

With Jay Michaels's help we had bridged the gap.

Look to World Markets

We learned very early that anything Americans had, the rest of the world was going to want. If signing up the Big Three was the luckiest thing we ever did, then setting up a bona fide network of international offices was the brightest. This was done in anticipation of the world demand for world-class athletes, but subsequent developments, such as satellite television, have made it look even smarter.

Today each of our fifteen full-time offices around the world is run and almost fully staffed by the nationality of the country in which it is located. We also share offices with local business partners in a dozen other countries.

Because of the flexibility and opportunities that these offices have given us, I am constantly amazed by the lack of attention and low priority most American companies give to their international divisions. If American companies spent as much time and effort selling their products overseas as they do in trying to keep foreign producers out, I think we'd see the flow of currency change direction overnight.

Charge for Your Expertise

Many companies fail to place a premium on the real dollar worth of their expertise, or what it would cost an outsider to learn what they already know. So did we for about ten years.

During that time we had been involved with more than a thousand companies in one sports promotion or another. We had amassed an enormous body of knowledge as to how companies should go about realizing their marketing goals through sports. And we often gave away this knowledge. If a company signed on John Newcombe and then didn't know how to use him, for everyone's sake we had to step in and show them.

By the early 1970s we recognized that more and more companies wanted to get into sports but had no idea how to do it. Their advertising agencies were not capable of intelligent advice in this area; their public relations firm didn't have a clue; and if they did get in it was usually because some high-ranking executive had a particular interest in a particular sport (usually the *worst* reason to get involved).

We finally began charging for our expertise. Today our corporate consulting division, Merchandising Consultants International (MCI), is our fastest growing company, as it was throughout most of the 1970s. MCI goes into a company and works with its marketing group to develop sports promotions that are not only cost-effective but have some *meaning* in terms of the company's specific objectives.

The demand has been even greater than we had anticipated. MCI lists more than one hundred corporations on its client roster, including many leaders of their respective industries, such as Sears, Kodak, R.J. Reynolds, AT&T, Seagram, Rolex, Hertz, Heinz, the Hearst Corporation, and Proctor & Gamble.

MCI's success, and the pedigree of its clients, suggested to us that there might be other ways to profit from our specialized expertise. This led us into the business of creating sports events and implementing them at an add-on cost or in exchange for a profit participation. These events are often televised, and when they are, we charge for this expertise as well.

This concept has led to the creation of the "Legends" men's and women's tennis tours, the World Championship of Women's Golf, the Pepsi Grand Slam, the World Triathlon Championships, and literally dozens of other tours and events.

If companies took the time to realize the true worth of their expertise, they could use it for growth opportunities which might otherwise be overlooked: as a separate profit center, such as we made of our consulting division; as an add-on to goods or services; as a sales incentive.

Even if you must give away your expertise as a price of doing business, it's helpful to know what it's really costing you—and it's helpful to let the buyer know as well.

Companies are often shy about doing this. It always reminds me of the story about the woman who approached Picasso in a restaurant, asked him to scribble something on a napkin, and said she would be happy to pay whatever he felt it was worth. Picasso complied and then said, "That will be $10,000."

"But you did that in thirty seconds," the astonished woman replied.

"No," Picasso said. "It has taken me forty years to do that."

Diversify Talent

Many companies will, as a matter of policy, shift their personnel from division to division. The idea behind this is that these employees will be motivated by new challenges and the divisions will benefit from a transfusion of new blood.

I think this policy fails on both counts. The employee either finds he is doing pretty much the same thing, only somewhere else in the chain of command, or something totally different, in which case his previous expertise is rendered useless. Meanwhile his former division finds it is always training people who will soon be gone.

We do it differently. When we take a new diversification step, or start a new business, we draw from our existing talent pool. Very often the employees tapped for these new responsibilities continue with some of their old responsibilities as well. Once they have become familiar with the new demands on their time, they hire the necessary support personnel or draw in additional talent from other divisions to deal with appropriate aspects of both their old and new responsibilities.

Our financial management division, for instance, has been called by *Money* magazine "arguably the best financial planners in America." Recently we began offering this service to corporations. As an added perk a company can pay us to do the personal financial management for its top executives.

Our people offering this service are the same people who manage Arnold Palmer's tax shelters, Bjorn Borg's real estate, Jackie Stewart's investments, and Alberto Salazar's and Sebastian Coe's trust funds (Salazar and Coe are still amateurs, and their income goes into a trust). The point is they will continue in this capacity, even with their formidable new responsibilities.

Apart from our consulting division (which must remain autonomous), I don't think we have one key employee who has only one job. Some of our key executives draw their paychecks from as many as six different divisions. It wreaks havoc on the flow charts, but it cuts down on job boredom, not to mention overhead. (I live in terror of Parkinson's law.) Employee motivation is one of the classic corporate problems I've never had to contend with. Everyone is too busy.

Take a Second Look at Timing

Timing, as we've seen, is critical to selling. For us, it has been even more significant as it relates to corporate growth.

When we began representing Jean Shrimpton in the late 1960s, I looked around and pretty much decided this was not a business we wanted to be in. Back then a good, hard-working model could earn $30,000–40,000 a year, with Shrimpton being perhaps the only exception.

Today models make $200,000–300,000 a year, and there are perhaps a dozen making much more. With licensing opportunities being what they are today, the superstars are earning—or should be earning—seven-figure incomes.

Modeling is a profession in which salaries have, one might say, exceeded inflation. And so we decided it was time to take a second look. Now that we have our marketing and licensing expertise, our many corporate affiliations, and our offices in all of the world's major fashion capitals, what hadn't made much sense orginally now made a whole lot of sense. Today we own Laraine Ashton, London's leading model agency, and Legends, the fastest growing agency in New York.

The same thing happened with team sports. We had dabbled in this area throughout the 1970s (the first million-dollar contract, Czonka/Kiick to the World Football League, was ours), but we had never made it a corporate priority.

Today a utility infielder or a place kicker can make several hundred thousand dollars. Moreover, judging from the success we've had in selling world television rights to NFL games, I predict we are not too far away from the day when income opportunities for football players will be available in Tokyo.

Two years ago we took a second look and began to strengthen our team sports division. By the end of 1985 we will be a major factor in this business and within the next five years the dominant factor in the business.

Short-Term Can Be Terminal

Over the years we have been fortunate enough and success-ful enough to contend with an interesting corporate problem: how to be profitable without being a profit-monger.

Personally, in any new business we have gone into, I become unhappy with anything less than a 100 percent market share. But corporately I'm smart enough to know that short-term greed is one of the biggest mistakes a company can make.

We have often been accused of trying to "take over" a sport, most notably golf, and then skiing and then tennis and now running. It hasn't happened, and we've been involved with golf for almost a quarter of a century.

In a sport such as tennis, where we represent many of its corporate sponsors, all merchandising and TV rights to Wimbledon, the television rights to the U.S. Open, and fifteen of the top twenty men and women players, and run numerous events and series of events, I have no doubt, if we wanted to, we could make an impact on the way the sport is structured and the way it is governed.

That would be very short-sighted. Our long-term interest is in enhancing any sport in which we are involved, doing everything we can to help it grow. This is not because we are "good sports" but because we are good businessmen.

Obviously, the growth of our business is linked, has always been linked, and will continue to be linked to the growth of sports. Right now I don't see that growth ending anytime soon, and any short-term gains we might make at the expense of the sport would be like killing our own golden goose.

Closely allied to this is another criticism we hear all the time, which is that we are guilty of conflict of interest. How can we fairly implement an event in which we represent the sponsors, the players, the television rights, and the governing body? The answer is . . . very carefully.

When the potential for a conflict of interest does indeed exist, we lay all our cards on the table. In fact, this sort of full disclosure is our protection. In every instance I can recall, we have demanded as a condition of our involvement that every party know what every other party was doing, that every party know where we were involved and how we were involved, and that every party understand that all disputes be resolved frontally and with the full participation and knowledge of everyone.

Ironically, we have lost several clients because they have "heard about" IMG's conflict of interest, but we have never lost a client because of conflict of interest.

If anything, I consider this charge something of a back-handed compliment. It's a sign that we've done a pretty good job of diversifying our experience.

12 Staying in Business

I REMEMBER HEARING A once-popular comedian talk about the dramatic rise and fall of his career: "You know the old adage, 'Be nice to people on the way up because you might meet them again on your way down'? Not true," he said. "On the way down you meet a totally different group." I have found something of the same thing to be true about building a business and running one. The problems you meet are totally different.

The overall problem is that everything becomes harder. It's harder to keep a company's momentum, to shift its speed, to alter its direction. It's harder to make decisions because so many additional factors have to be considered, and it's harder to get them executed because you are rarely talking directly to the people who will be executing them.

But the biggest single problem, by far, is that the structures and systems created to make all this a little easier, to make it all flow a little smoother, begin to stifle the very momentum they are supposed to help.

The Nature of Systems

Ben Bidwell, now the executive vice-president of Chrysler and the former head of North American sales for the Ford Motor Company, once described to me Ford's structure—and the systems created to support it—as a "wall of molasses. You can't get anything in. You can't get anything out. You can't move up. You can't move sideways. It takes two years even to move down."

I think this was less a comment on Ford than on the nature of any mature organization. During the period of rapid growth, when a company may be doubling or tripling in size each year, the growth itself tends to make the structures less constrictive. But as a company matures, and as its growth rate settles in to a steady 15 or 20 percent a year, systems and structures are allowed to take root, and like weeds in a garden they begin to choke the life out of the organizations that seeded them.

This is the sinister, uncompromising nature of systems. They ride roughshod over everything, especially common sense, and are the single biggest reason why working for a company can often be a ludicrous experience. It takes forever to get something into the system, and once it is in it is almost impossible to get it back out.

John DeLorean told me that shortly after he had become general manager of Chevrolet he attended a sales conference in Dallas, and when he arrived at his hotel suite he discovered that someone from the company had delivered a huge basket of fruit to his room. Remarking to an associate on the basket's size and variety he commented, humorously, he thought, "What? No bananas?"

From that moment on, the word throughout General Motors was "John DeLorean loves bananas." No matter how many times he attempted to explain that he had only meant to be amusing, bananas kept showing up in cars, chartered planes, hotel suites—even in meetings—and followed him throughout his career at Chevrolet.

Another problem with systems is that responsibility is passed along and down and around, and eventually, when it finally reaches the guy who is actually supposed to do something, someone has invariably forgotten to tell him the reason.

In the early 1970s one of Arnold Palmer's endorsees was Lincoln Mercury, and I told Gar Laux, then the general manager of Lincoln Mercury, that if he was interested we could arrange to use a couple of Lincolns as the photographic backdrop in a forthcoming series of Arnold's print ads for his apparel licensee, Robert Bruce.

Gar was delighted by this opportunity for "free" advertising and said, "Just let us know when and where you want the cars and we'll make sure they get there."

Several weeks later, the head of our apparel division received a call from a lower-echelon Lincoln Mercury executive who wanted to know where the cars should be sent and what colors they should be. "Bermuda, three weeks from today," our executive told him, but as to color, which really didn't matter, he said, "I don't know. Whatever you have. What about a navy and a maroon?"

Several days before the shoot, our apparel executive received a call from a different employee at Lincoln Mercury who this time wanted to know precisely where in Bermuda the cars should be shipped. "We've had to charter a plane," he said, "because our Bermuda dealer doesn't have a blue or a maroon car. In fact," he added, "there's only one of each on the Eastern seaboard, and the plane first has to fly to Boston to pick up the maroon car and then to Washington to get the navy blue."

Most of the best-run companies are not only aware of these sorts of system-created problems, but focus much of their management energy on breaking the stranglehold. Perhaps this is where I could have benefited from a Harvard M.B.A., because nobody told us this. We had to figure it out for ourselves.

Think Small

In our formative years there was so much going on, so much to do, we really didn't have time to think that much about systems, organization, and structure, and we didn't really have to. Things just seemed to get done, and getting them done under conditions of barely organized chaos probably added to the excitement.

But it was becoming increasingly obvious that we couldn't continue to operate that way, especially after we began to diversify. I realized the nature of my job was changing as well and was likely to change even more. I was also spending more of my time on administration and less and less on everything else.

In order to alleviate some of this administrative burden, in order to eliminate some of the chaos, and in order to grow and expand in some sensible systematic manner, coming up with a structural framework became a major priority.

When we first sat down to discuss structure and organization, I knew that while we weren't going to stay small, I wanted to preserve what I could of the "small feeling" we had when we started out.

There is no other feeling like that in business, or at least any that I have ever experienced. It's not just the excitement, although that is certainly part of it. It is more a sense of the immediacy and importance that everything takes on, the feeling that what you do from day to day *matters,* and that generates a desire to do even more.

It also brings with it a certain amount of anxiety. It's hard to feel complacent in a tiny new company because in the back of your mind you're always wondering whether you're still going to be around in six months. It puts an edge on everything you do. I wanted, if possible, to avoid a bureaucratic structure that would dull this edge.

There is also an esprit in small, growing companies which is difficult to explain to anyone who has never experienced it. I suspect it is not unlike the feeling one gets from being a member of a champion sports team, a satisfaction that comes from contributing to something larger than yourself. In the early days, when Arnold or Gary would win a tournament over the weekend, everyone would come in to work so pumped up Monday morning there would literally be races for the telephones. I knew, however, that if we were to grow we would soon have people working for us who wouldn't know a putter from a wedge, much less who won over the weekend.

I knew this special esprit could not be totally preserved, but certainly part of it could, and I wanted a structure that would help us achieve that. The key, I felt, was to think small, to structure something that would make everyone feel like a very big cog in his or her respective wheel.

Our response was to organize the company into a group of twelve smaller companies, each functioning as a separate autonomous profit center but each with additional responsibilities to other companies within the group and to the group at large as well. The primary responsibility of our golf company, for instance, was representing our professional golf clients. Yet its overall responsibilities included any golf-related activities, which translated into specific functions within several of our other companies, including fashion, television, financial management, and publishing.

I felt this structure would lend a sense of immediacy and importance to everyone's role within the company. As we grew, I also felt the interconnections would reduce the need for more and more layers of management to coordinate these various intragroup activities.

The result was a structure that looked less like a single pyramid than a row of small pyramids. In the beginning some of these pyramids were *very small,* consisting of one executive and a secretary. As we have grown, one of these original companies became a staff function and others have been subdivided into additional companies or new autonomous divisions. But otherwise they function pretty much today as they were conceived back then.

Don't Let Structures Run the Operation

The fluidity of business is simply too fast and too formless for existing systems and structures to hold it. Once our structures were in place we began an ongoing process of ignoring them. I believe this is one of the greatest challenges to almost any established company—a constant recognition that you often have to jump out of existing structures in order to let new business in.

I understand that this is the way IBM developed its Peanut computer. They took some of their brightest minds, put them outside existing structures and rules, and told them to get on with it. I suspect most revolutionary technological and business advancements were created outside, or substantially outside, an existing structure.

I am often confronted by executives in our own company who would like nothing more than to have everything neatly compartmentalized. Even if they recognize the validity of what is being discussed or understand the larger picture, their minds demand order and conformity to the systems, and their "yes" is invariably followed by a "but": "Yes, *but* whose budget will this come out of?" "Yes, *but* where am I going to get the manpower?" "Yes, *but* who's going to oversee it?" I suppose there were a lot of division managers at IBM who went into a mild state of shock when informed that their number two or three guy was being plucked away for some special project.

But good management must resist both the internal and external pressures to force new business into the old holes, simply because those holes already exist. Once a company allows structure to run its operation, it is only a few missed opportunities away from total stagnation.

Think Flexibility

You have to sell the flexibility of the structure to the people who work for you, and the only way to do this is by deeds rather than words. Your employees have to see the tangible proof not only that the structure is flexible but that this flexibility works to their advantage and their self-interest.

This was one of our considerations in the initial line structuring of our organization. I wanted to be able to pull two people from company A and two people from company B to start company C, or to take someone from company C to head up a special project affecting companies A, B, and C.

However, I also wanted the people within the structure to *feel* this flexibility. I wanted them to know that we were going to try out good ideas, no matter who thought of them, no matter how directly or indirectly these ideas applied to their division or to their specific areas of responsibilities. I also wanted them to know that if someone came up with a good workable idea that idea was not simply going to be handed over to someone else. Whoever conceived it would be involved in its execution.

Our entry into the creation, implementation, and televising of specialized sports events has given us our best opportunity for doing this, for *showing* the system's flexibility and letting those within the system *feel* it. These events often involve a coordinated effort among five or six of our companies. Each event varies from the next, and though we have now created more than fifty events, we have yet to create a structure to define what they are, who's doing them, or how they are supposed to work.

Last year one of those events was a Masters of Hockey contest, which pitted a team of Hockey Hall of Famers against a team of former Boston Bruins stars. It was staged at a jam-packed, sold-out Boston Gardens, and while the event was administered by our team sports division, which also provided the players, the idea itself came from one of our tennis executives, who was made responsible for its overall execution.

Because we are always practicing flexibility rather than preaching it, I suspect we are less a victim of our own systems than many companies are. Recently, when I told Ben Bidwell that I was working on a book of business advice, he said, "Mark, you only have one secret: IMG spends 90 percent of its time on business and 10 percent on organization."

Reserve the Right to Be Arbitrary

As chairman, president, and CEO of IMG, I reserve the right to be arbitrary. Because of the way our company is structured and the flexibility and fluidity I try to maintain, I exercise this right with some regularity.

Our executives will often balk at a decision I have made because it doesn't seem fair or because it violates certain assumptions they have made about how the company works. I have, on occasion, made decisions or proposed solutions which were equally unsatisfactory to all parties.

Yet I can think of many reasons why I reserve this right and hundreds of situations where I have had to exercise it. I may know certain facts that totally alter the face of a situation, and yet the time has not come to share these facts with others. I may have to make a decision which is good for the group in the long term but may penalize one of our companies in the short run. Sometimes the decision affects something we will definitely be doing in the future. Sometimes it affects something we may or may not be doing in the future but is needed to give us the option.

I must reserve the right to be arbitrary because, as CEO, one of my prime responsibilities to the company itself, and by extension to the people who work for it, is to provide awareness for growth and protect the future. And the best decisions for doing this are not always the fairest or the most popular.

Don't Let Policies Stifle the Operation

If structures create a drag on business momentum, then outdated, outmoded policies create a drag on the business itself. This seems obvious to me. Yet on countless occasions I have run into corporations in which some ridiculously restrictive policy prevented them from doing something they actually wanted to do. I have seen chairmen of boards, when pressed for the reasons behind some of these policies, shrug their shoulders and confess they didn't remember, or wonder out loud why such a policy ever existed in the first place.

I recently read that a jogger in Palm Beach, Florida, was arrested for jogging on a street that ran north and south. Apparently some town ordinance which had been on the books for more than fifty years permitted running *only* on east–west thoroughfares.

Little tidbits like this pop up every now and then in the newspapers. Someone discovers some obscure, ancient county or state ordinance which prohibits public gum chewing or singing in elevators. We laugh at the absurdity of these laws and wonder how anyone ever thought them up. Yet I would venture there are rules which are equally absurd and equally outdated in the corporate policy manuals of many major American corporations.

A company's unofficial policies can be just as bizarre and even more damaging. Policies are the day-to-day laws of the corporation. The danger you run with unofficial policies is that people may follow them.

I have a friend who runs a small business. His unofficial

policy is to pay all creditors within fifteen business days. He was attempting to buy into another business and had secured a substantial loan from the bank for this purpose. He was in Europe when the loan arrived, and when he returned to his office three weeks later he discovered his accounting department had paid off every outstanding invoice—with the money he had just borrowed from the bank.

The corporate policies which I often find to be the most short-sighted are the "precedent policies," whereby a company's desire to protect a minor precedent will result in the loss of a major opportunity.

When we were attempting to negotiate Arnold's equipment contract with Wilson Sporting Goods back in the early 1960s, my counterparts at Wilson and I had spent a great deal of time coming up with an insurance clause we all felt we could live with. But someone at Wilson suggested that this clause would never get approved by Judge Cooney, the Wilson Meat Packing Company's crochety old boss, because it was unprecedented; if they approved this for Arnold, they would have to offer the same plan to all Wilson employees. (Our insurance man answered with a wonderful letter suggesting that Wilson *should* offer this plan to all qualifying employees, the qualification being that they win the Masters and the U.S. Open in the same year!)

As it turned out, the Wilson guy was right. Judge Cooney refused to sign the new contract, and the insurance clause was one of the main reasons. This enabled Arnold to get out of his agreement with Wilson and to found his own sporting goods company. I would guess that precedent has cost Wilson millions of dollars.

The most bizarre encounter I have ever had with another company's policies occurred in the early 1970s.

General Motors had a rule against any direct financial involvement in the sport of motor racing.

Pete Estes, who was general manager of Chevrolet at the time (he later became GM's chairman), and Chevrolet's agency, Campbell-Ewald, had been working with us for almost six months to finalize a very complex deal with Jean-Claude Killy. The core of the agreement was a television series starring Killy which Chevrolet would sponsor but which involved a number of other contractual obligations as well, including a commitment from Killy to drive a Corvette in the most famous of all endurance races, the 24-Hours of Le Mans.

Killy had actually become quite excited about this particular commitment when I began to hear rumblings out of Detroit that all was not well at Chevrolet.

Word had come down from the chairman of GM that under no circumstances was Killy to get behind the wheel of a Corvette at Le Mans, that if necessary Chevrolet was to pay off the agreement in full and cancel it. Chevrolet was quite embarrassed by this and offered to commit to six additional television shows, to honor all its other commitments, and even to finance Killy's Le Mans race—as long as he did not drive a Corvette or any other General Motors product.

Killy participated in Le Mans that year and fulfilled his commitment to Chevrolet—by driving a Porsche.

Manage Unconventionally

Managing a mature company is not just a constant process of breaking out of archaic structures and antiquated policies. You also have to be consciously, actively, and aggressively punching holes in the company's conventions and conventional wisdom.

It's too easy to say, "It's worked this way before," or "This is how we've always done it." It's too easy to get mentally locked in, to reject automatically a fresh or new approach.

Companies, by nature, are conservative. People resist change, particularly in the working environment. They would like to feel the company they are working for now will look pretty much the same five years from now.

This is why breaking out is always a fight. You are going against the grain. The irony is that a mature company gains momentum by pushing against the flow of the existing momentum.

Have you noticed that the best-run companies all seem to be managed unconventionally? Every time they are written up or profiled in a business magazine, their success is attributed to breaking the rules, not following them; encouraging employee, departmental, and divisional independence, not stifling it; bursting through the conventional wisdom, not perpetuating it.

Manage unconventionally. Don't just look for opportunities to do the unexpected. Create them. Aggressively pursue change. Make managing an active verb.

Recently I had occasion to replace the head of one of our most important divisions, international television sales, which includes the licensing of television rights to many of the world's major sporting events. There were a number of qualified candidates within our television company, but I chose an executive from our skiing division.

It was an opportunity to try something new, to do the unexpected, and in the eighteen months since, the profits in that division have substantially increased.

Manage with Confidence

It is the ability to delegate which, more than anything else, separates the good managers from the bad ones.

Delegation is the process of building up people, then letting go of a responsibility. It sounds easy, but it almost never is. Egos get in the way. People would rather be perceived as the authority than support the authority or expertise of the people who work for them.

It is also difficult to let go of a responsibility. Again, it's often a matter of ego. People convince themselves that they can do something better than anyone else, or are afraid that if they give up a task or responsibility they will be perceived as being less essential to the company.

It takes a very confident person to be a good manager, confidence in the people who work for you and enough confidence in yourself to overcome these ego problems.

It is human nature to want to see the fruits of your labor, to feel the dirt between your fingers, to perform tasks which not only produce tangible results but which are themselves tangible. Managers must seek a different kind of satisfaction. They have got to be able to build up people and give them responsibilities, to find ego gratification in training, directing, and overseeing others.

Delegate What You Can, Not What You Want To

We have several executives who are still performing certain tasks which should have been delegated to others a long time ago. These tasks are not the best use of these executives' time, they all could be performed equally well by people working for them . . . and they all involve spending several days several times a year in a resortlike area for the purposes of entertaining corporate clients or producing some of our television shows. As far as I'm concerned, these aren't "tasks" at all but corporate perks that these executives have awarded themselves.

The reverse of this is even more common. In fact, there is an expression about the tendency of certain viscous matter to flow downhill that is used to describe it. Freely translated, it says: "The more distasteful a task, the further down it is going to be delegated." One of Federal Express's early television commercials showed a package being handed down from one level of a company to the next until the person with the final responsibility for mailing it was five or six people removed from the person who was sending it. The first time I saw that commercial I remember thinking I'm glad I'm not the guy on top of *that* totem pole.

People will often delegate—or fail to delegate—for all the wrong reasons. They hold on to a task because they like doing it, or want to do it, or are afraid not to do it, and they will pass down some other task because they find it distasteful or "beneath them" or have rationalized that it is not the best use of their time.

All sorts of business considerations have to be weighed when determining what should and should not be delegated.

During the early years of my representation of Arnold Palmer, if he wanted a pair of golf shoes sent to him in Houston he would not call the shoe manufacturer, he would not call the director of our golf or apparel divisions, he would not call his secretary or my secretary. He would call me. And for reasons of loyalty, and the ongoing importance of our relationship, I took care of it.

I mentioned this one day to Lew Wasserman, chairman of MCA and one of my early business mentors, and I was happily surprised when he said that, indeed, that was the way it should be. "When Jules Stein founded MCA back in 1924," Wasserman said, "his first client was bandleader Guy Lombardo. Thirty years later, under Jules's leadership, MCA had grown into the world's largest entertainment company. But when Lombardo called, Jules would still handle it personally. We would be waiting for a board meeting to start, and Jules would be on the phone with Guy Lombardo, discussing what arrangement he should play that night from the rooftop room at the Roosevelt Hotel in New Orleans."

Hire People Smarter than Yourself

Wasserman and I continued talking about how MCA had grown into a billion-dollar corporation, how IMG might also be able to grow, and by extension, how an understanding of delegation would make that happen.

As we took on new clients, I could not be expected personally to handle the golf shoes, the tennis racquets, or the skis for all of them. This seemed fairly obvious, but when you are discussing representation with athletes who are the best in the world at their particular sports it may not seem so obvious to them. *"Hire people who are smarter than you are,"* Wasserman said to me, *"then don't sell yourself, sell your company."*

Obviously, I don't believe that everyone we've ever hired is smarter than I, but I can honestly say that I would not want to match my expertise in fashion, tennis, television, skiing, or football against the people who are running these divisions for us. And I truly do believe that the clients being represented by these divisions are in much better hands than if I was representing them personally. This is what makes it easy for me now to sell my company rather than myself.

One of the difficulties with delegation is that managers will sometimes paint themselves as the experts rather than as expert managers. Sell your division rather than yourself, and you will find more of a willingness among others outside your company to work with your subordinates. The smarter you make the people who work for you look, the smarter you are going to look as a manager. It's also less masochistic.

Take Five Hours to Save Five Minutes

Several months ago I participated in a pro–am tennis exhibition. Just before we were to go on the court, I happened to overhear a conversation between our opponents. The pro, who was one of the top-ranked players in the world, said to his amateur partner, "Do you want to win this match or do you just want to play some tennis?"

The amateur, who was a little intimidated, replied rather sheepishly, "Well, I guess I would like to win the match."

"Fine," the pro said. "Then serve and get off the court!"

This may have been the way for the pro to win that particular match, but it is hardly the best strategy for building a strong doubles team against tough competition over the long term.

I chuckled to myself at the time, but aren't there a lot of people in business guilty of this same attitude? They would rather do it themselves than take the time to teach someone else to do it for them. They feel they could be most effective if everyone else would just get out of their way.

I recently asked one of our executives how a new employee he had hired was getting along. "He'll work out just fine," he said, "but right now it's frustrating. It takes me five hours to show him something I could do myself in five minutes."

That one statement underscores:

- The biggest stumbling block to delegation
- A big reason for unfounded resentment toward subordinates
- The importance of training
- The need to *keep* a trained employee
- A good reason why companies don't grow

Fortunately, even though it was frustrating him, this particular executive understood the mathematics of delegation. Five hours now could save him hundreds of hours in the future.

So many people in management fail to appreciate this very simple arithmetic. Either they underestimate the importance of training or lack the patience to deal with it. Some managers, I believe, don't understand that in teaching someone else to do the job they are doing they are freeing up their own time for more important tasks and greater responsibilities.

These managers are usually the ones who end up staying in a company's middle echelons. They are too busy doing all the other jobs they should have trained others to do and too "valuable" doing them to take on any larger roles in their companies.

Management Philosophies That Don't Work— and One That Does

Most management philosophy that you read in a book or learn in a classroom is going to have limited effectiveness. Once you factor in human beings—egos and personalities— even the most sensible theories begin to fall apart. It is like the ancient children's game, Paper, Scissors, Stone. Management philosophies and management theories are always topped by Real Life.

The only management philosophy that does work is the one that acknowledges that none of them do: Be flexible and strive for consistency.

Flexibility is probably the one word that most closely defines my approach to management. I have found that as soon as I begin to accept anything as gospel I run into the heretics—people or pieces of information that burst my comfortable convictions.

If IMG had adhered to the gospel as we know it, we

would not be in the modeling agency business today, nor would we have our team sports division.

But flexibility is not just rethinking your business. It must extend to all aspects of management, from how often you reevaluate policies to how receptive you are to listening to what your employees are telling you.

As a company, we are so decentralized and scattered around the world that for a couple of years all our executives were required to submit weekly activity reports, similar to time sheets kept by lawyers, with copies going to all parties with a need to know. I felt this was a pretty good idea, and still feel it is, but what I found out was that there was a tremendous resistance to these reports. They were time-consuming, and because a few executives began to use them as weapons, others began to feel the need to cover themselves. What began as a good idea became a terrible one. So we made them bimonthly. Flexibility may be more than just a management "approach." If you're responsive to the people who work for you, it may be an obligation.

Manage for Consistency

Most companies, I assume, would prefer to grow steadily at a healthy rate rather than doubling in size one year and losing money the next. No one can manage this kind of schizophrenia effectively with any long-term success, and no one should try. Next to profitability, the most important goal a company should strive for is consistency.

If flexibility is the means, then consistency—of performance and growth—is the end. This sounds like something of a contradiction. If one is being flexible how can one be consistent? In fact, not only are they compatible, but a flexible, responsive management virtually guarantees consistency. It is inflexibility that causes erratic behavior. A company goes on for too long adhering to all the old rules and outdated modes of performance. Then one morning someone wakes up, panics, overreacts, and throws out *all* the rules. That can make people nuts.

To manage consistently you have to behave consistently. Even if people don't like what you are saying, they still want to know where you are coming from.

I have tried to be consistent in emphasizing what I think is important and what I think is insignificant. There's a certain solace in that. Inconsistency in management breeds all sorts of unnecessary anxieties in the people being managed. There are enough legitimate anxieties in business without adding to them by not letting people know where you are coming from.

There are any number of things that the people who work for me don't like about the way I run my company, and I'm sure this is true of any company that hasn't been thoroughly committee-ized and is still being run by a boss. But the things they don't like now are pretty much the same things they didn't like ten years ago.

Dealing with Employees

The whole idea of managing for consistency brings up another seeming contradiction which, to me anyway, embodies the "artistic" aspect of management: What happens when policy meets personality?

Much has been said and written lately about the success of "people-oriented" companies. These companies talk a lot about being part of the "team" or "family" and have slogans like "People first, then profits." Obviously, you manage through people, but implicit in this approach is the idea that you always get the most out of people through positive motivation.

I don't buy this, and I suspect a lot of other people who

would like to believe it don't buy it either. If everyone were the same, if everyone responded to the same carrot, then this would make more sense. But it doesn't ring true because it is only half the solution.

In the real world, no two people are motivated in precisely the same way or by exactly the same things, and no individual works on a totally even keel. Even the steadiest performers have their ups and downs.

I have four general philosophies for dealing with employees: (1) Pay them what they are worth; (2) Make them feel that they are important, yet (3) Make them think for themselves; and (4) Separate office life from social life.

Pay Them What They Are Worth

Very few people are worth very much to a company at the beginning. Everyone is being overpaid, but the overpayment is an investment in the person and in the future. We do not pay people well to begin with—we want them to prove themselves. We pay very well after they have proven themselves. Since I was fortunate enough to make pretty good money at a fairly young age, I have no psychological hang-ups about the people who work for me making a lot of money at a very young age. Before they do, however, I want them to perform well and to be deserving of it.

It is important to split away the ego factor in salary levels from true worth and real contribution. It is equally important to make the employee realize that this is what you are doing and to make the employee realize further the value of his job. If, for example, a corporate policy gives bonuses secured from airline travel while on company business and the employee is free to use these airline bonuses for himself or his family, then make sure he knows that this is part of his compensation. Be sure that if an employee ties a vacation into a business trip that he knows the value of that or, conversely, what the vacation would have cost had there not been a business trip. Do not let an employee forget these examples when he starts saying, "All I am making from this job is x dollars."

I strive to keep a dynamic interaction going between myself and the people who work for me. As an employer, I have always tried to be generous with people in the area of fringe benefits, but I want both of us to know that I am being generous.

Make Them Feel That They Are Important—Yet Motivate, Both Positively and Negatively

It is very important to build employees up, make them feel important, and let them get credit for things that they have accomplished. It is important that you give them this credit directly and openly to their peers and to the outside world. As you do this, however, it is important to teach them the "we" of the situation. Motivate them to keep selling the company while at the same time taking credit for their particular accomplishment. There is nothing worse than an executive who tries to take credit personally for something his subordinates or assistants have done.

While being free with your praise, never let people rest on their laurels, and feel that a good accomplishment one week allows them to get away with almost anything in future weeks.

Sometimes you can motivate good employees to be better by pointing out their minor shortcomings and urging them to even greater heights. This is what I call negative motivation.

In the real world part of "playing for a winner," as any football coach can tell you, sometimes means bolstering a team's self-confidence and sometimes means bringing the players down a couple of notches. Sometimes it can mean straight intimidation: "Do you measure up?" "Are you good enough to play for this team?"

As in most companies, our employees have more than one job, more than one area of responsibility. If one of our executives is feeling pretty terrific about something, I'll sometimes tend to bring up one of those areas where things aren't going so well. If he's down on himself, it's easy enough for me to find something he's doing right.

People who really care about what they do—and I think most of our executives are in that category—tend to work in emotional peaks and valleys. Consistency of management and consistency of performance is achieved by filling in those valleys and lopping off a peak every now and then.

I think it is important to keep your employees slightly off balance, even at the cost of occasional unfairness. I think it is important to make people aware of their mistakes, even if this means some occasional second-guessing.

One of the biggest enemies of established companies is complacency. You have to keep the edge in, and when the people who work for you feel too secure or too self-satisfied, that is when you lose the edge.

As an employer I want people to feel they have to measure up, to be "good enough" to work for us. If someone is particularly pleased with a deal he or she has done, I will commend that employee for it but I might also say, "Who has foreign rights?" or "Why didn't we do such-and-such?" or bring up something else that will send them away thinking, "Why didn't I think of that?" and leave them a little less complacent, overconfident, or self-satisfied.

Obviously there are times when you have to do just the opposite. There are times when you have to build people up, give them a pat on the back, and help them put things in perspective.

I spoke not too long ago with one of our executives who had really been having a streak of bad luck. One of his clients, a leading athlete, had been threatening to leave for about six months. And he had just returned from the Orange Bowl football game, where he had gone to sign up Nebraska's Heisman Trophy winner, Mike Rozier. We had received verbal commitments from him and family members, but, although subsequently denied by the player, it appeared that he had accepted money from another agent who could have exposed this fact if Rozier did not sign with him.

Needless to say the executive, who had spent months pursuing Rozier and had done everything in the proper and ethical way, was devastated. When I spoke to him I pointed out that he should be pleased with his effort regardless of the results, that we were not going to get down in the gutter with anyone, and that the admirable way in which he had conducted himself was of far greater value to the company.

Make Them Think for Themselves

The "Kinda-Sorta" School of Management. Very often people say that my "management style," if you want to call it that, is to encourage all of our employees at all levels to think for themselves. I believe in this one; it goes straight to the bottom line.

When one of our executives comes to me with a specific problem or question, I'll often answer nonspecifically: "When we did the such-and-such deal with so-and-so we kinda said that if they could do this then we might be able to do that. Isn't there a way that we can kinda do that sorta thing here?"

With due acknowledgment to Socrates and the Harvard Business School, it kinda works.

Very recently we were trying to sign a British television personality, and the executive in charge of the project was having some difficulties in negotiating the specific points because the prospective client was raising a lot of objections to our fees. The executive asked me how I thought he should handle it. I suggested three or four approaches, ranging from conceding to taking a hard line and risking losing the client, and then I suggested that there had been times in the past when we knew that we would do a good job and we told the client, "Let's not resolve the fee now. Let's work it out in a while when we've worked for you, and you can pay us what you think it's worth."

From the way I presented it, it was pretty clear that this was the way I felt he should approach the problem, but I left the decision of how to approach the problem in such a way that he believed that it was his solution not mine.

We signed the client.

Separate Office Life from Social Life

My overriding philosophy on this one is to minimize the relations outside of the office. I will never forget when Arnold Palmer, who is just about as nice a person as you will ever want to meet, had a pilot who was really a very good pilot but not exactly the sort of person you wanted to spend your evenings with, let alone have attend business meetings with you. Arnold, however, could not bring himself to tell the pilot he would see him the next day, since he thought that was not being very nice and that the pilot would somehow be offended. Then came a meeting with a golf game manufacturer from Kansas City and the pilot attended—and started making comments about the nature of the game and the sort of contract that there ought to be. I will never forget the expression on Arnold's face. Needless to say, it was the last time that the pilot spent evenings with us or attended meetings.

Socializing within the office is certainly better not done than done. In the very early days of IMG, when we were only a very few, we just plain did not permit it. Times change and the work changes and there is very little that one can do to forbid it on any level. It does, however, create a lot of very obvious problems.

It is impossible to let your hair down with someone one evening and try to be completely yourself if the next day you have got to reprimand, fire, reassign, or in some other way interact on a business basis with that person. Nor can the employee turn off from the night before to the next day.

As a general rule, one is better off by miles not complicating a business relationship within the company by all sorts of undercurrents from various social interactions. When somebody is having a relationship, it opens an entire range of confidentiality problems, for the personal relationship in all but a few circumstances will override the business situation and confidentiality.

Firing People

There are many ways to fire people. Henry Ford told Bunkie Knudsen, "It just didn't work out," and a couple of years later allegedly said to Lee Iacocca, "I just don't like you." Bill Paley of CBS reportedly decided one day that his whiz-kid programmer, Jim Aubrey, was "just not the kind of guy I want to run this company when I retire."

These firings were sudden and unexpected, which, totally apart from the question of their legitimacy, is cause enough to question how they were handled. Whenever I hear that someone has been fired out of the blue, I suspect it is emotional overreaction rather than the result of a considered business judgment.

When I know I will have to fire a particular person, I consider two factors—timing and that person's loyalty to the company.

You must fire someone when it hurts you the least both externally and internally. This can be anywhere from immediately to, in one case I can recall, two years later. As a general rule in our business, where relationships with clients can often be strong and personal, a certain amount of preparation is usually necessary.

One must also be sensitive to the feelings of the person

being fired—helping him or her to save face. The degree to which I take this into account is determined by that person's loyalty and service to the company.

Before firing people who have been loyal, you owe it to them first to exhaust all other possibilities—a lateral shift, the creation of a new job more compatible to their skills, even a disguised demotion. If no such avenue exists, then you must give them time to "adjust" to the idea of being fired and do whatever you can to help them find another job.

In several instances I have fired people without their even knowing it. Instead I have found jobs for them and let another company "steal them away."

On the other end of the spectrum, if I have good reason to believe that an employee is either disloyal or can't be trusted, then I will get him out of the company as quickly and as efficiently as I can.

We once had an employee who, I discovered, was planning to leave anyway and was going to take with him everything he could—clients, files, and any confidential information he could lay his hands on. I also had reason to believe that he would be vindictive and, once he was fired, would do whatever he could on the outside to hurt us. It took us about two weeks to protect our flanks. We arranged for this employee to take a one-day trip to Detroit. While he was gone, we had the locks changed and his files and records removed, and when he returned we fired him.

The vindictive factor alone is enough to make firing anyone a careful and considered judgment, and companies should be cautious about burning their bridges. A bitter exemployee can do great harm. He is considered a credible source to the outside world even if what he is saying totally lacks credibility.

But when people feel they have been fired "fairly"—treated with dignity, respect, and sensitivity in what, by definition, is a demeaning experience—they will be reluctant to bad-mouth their excompany. And they just may—as has happened to us on several occasions—become valued future business associates.

Consultants

If your company has hired a consultant (financial, management, whatever) and you are not taking his advice—fire him.

This is no reflection on the consultant. He may be giving you the best advice you will ever get, but if you are not following it you are wasting his time and your money.

Lead by Example

I suppose I am not the easiest person in the world to work for. I can be very demanding of our management executives. But I am also very demanding of myself.

If you ask a subordinate to come in at seven in the morning or stay until ten at night, he or she is going to be a lot less reluctant to do this if he knows that you have gotten up at five that morning or will be staying until eleven that night yourself. If you call that same employee from a yacht on the French Riviera and suggest the same thing, it's probably going to leave a different impression.

Just because it's a cliché doesn't mean it's any less true: Don't demand from your employees anything that you aren't demanding from yourself.

Ignore the Doomsayers

Companies can sometimes get into new businesses for defensive reasons—to protect their flanks or as an overreaction to competition.

Every company has its corporate doomsayers who will try to get you to do exactly this. They will say, "If we don't get into such-and-such a business, then all sorts of terrible things are going to happen. We're probably too late as it is." Obviously, these people don't have the interest of the company at heart. They are only interested in creating can't-lose situations for themselves: They have already taken credit for anticipated success, and they've already covered themselves for anticipated failure.

When the reasons are defensive it almost never works. You know going in that the effort is going to be greater than the rewards, which in itself creates a self-fulfilling failure.

Frank Bennack, president and CEO of Hearst, told me that a few years ago he was having to resist all sorts of internal pressure to get into the video games business. Video games were the future, he was told, and for a communications/entertainment company not to have a position in this industry would be a disaster.

Much to his credit, he resisted. If he had listened to the doomsayers, today Hearst would be giving away some version of "Donkey Kong" with a subscription to *Good Housekeeping.*

Get Beneath the Party Line

Several years ago, Chris Lewinton, managing director of Wilkinson Sword, gave me some very good advice about running a company. "Get to know the people two levels down from you," he said. "That's where your future is going to be, and it will give a better idea about the present."

CEOs, and managers on down the line, can often become isolated from what is really going on in their own companies. They talk to the same people over and over again, usually numbers one and two in each division. Generally the manager and his assistant will share the same viewpoint. They will make decisions together and sell those decisions together to upper management.

But getting to know the people one level below that can be an eye-opener. They will often have a refreshingly different take on what is going on and on what you are being told. These views may be slanted, or just as self-serving as anyone else's, but it helps to have a range of viewpoints rather than the same old party line.

Go for Profit

Samuel Johnson once said, "There are few ways in which a man can be more innocently employed than in getting money."

Maybe the largest problem of established companies is their bigness. The bigger the company, the easier it is to get off on tangents and forget why you are in business in the first place, which is to make a profit.

I have an acquaintance who started a fabulously successful business which literally grew exponentially—nearly 6000 percent—during its first eight years. Almost overnight he was beset by all the problems this out-of-control growth creates, and he began to experiment with all sorts of solutions, from bringing in a new management team, to totally restructuring the company, to getting out of certain aspects of his business, to selling it and getting out entirely. As you might expect, he went through a couple of very bad years while these experiments were going on.

When I saw him about a year later I was surprised to learn that he had turned the business totally around and was projecting profits that year to be up 100 percent. When I asked him how he had achieved this he spoke about some of the new people he had hired and some of the structural changes he had made. "But," he said, "I guess the biggest reason is that we doubled our prices."

Getting back to profitability may not always be this simple, but sometimes it's a lot less complicated than all the professionals would lead you to believe.

Recently I came across an article on Schlumberger Ltd., the oil well testing operation, which is one of the biggest, best-run, and most profitable companies in the world. Schlumberger publicizes to its customers that its service is marked up 100 percent. If Schlumberger's costs go up, so does their cost to the customer, and not by the same amount, but by double that amount. They not only remember to make a profit; they are not afraid to make one.

Sometimes the answer may be that simple: Charge more. Or at least charge enough so that you are not always losing money.

Many companies, I believe, who are busy buying new businesses and bringing in new management teams haven't even tested the outside edge of their profitability.

I see this all the time in our business. I see our executives afraid to ask what we are really worth or having trouble asking for expenses in addition to fees. They are simply afraid to test the outside edge of what someone might be willing to pay. (I once had a secretary in London who couldn't even *bill* what someone was willing to pay. She attended to the business affairs and became very good friends with two young British golf clients. She really knocked herself out for these clients and did a lot of little extras for them, which is good business. But two years later I noticed we had never collected our fees from them. When I asked her about it, she blushed and said she just couldn't bring herself to talk to them about money!)

The Danger of the Big Kill

The danger of the "big kill" is to an established business what the danger of growing too quickly is to a new one. In theory, most companies would like to double their profits in a year. However, few could really handle it, and most well-run companies wouldn't even try. One of the ways businesses lose profits is to fall prey to the big-kill syndrome. Big companies, burdened by large overheads, commit to deals that they know going in are at best break-even propositions. These companies need to learn to say no.

This is particularly true of businesses that rely on government contracts. In their effort to win a bidding war they will take on a project which doubles their overhead and makes no significant contributions to profitability. Several years later when the project is finished they either go bankrupt or they take on even bigger break-even propositions.

Corporations will often use their fear of this to justify diversification. However, intelligent diversification requires so many other considerations that I've never felt this to be a valid response.

Whom Are You Trying to Impress?

To me, one of the most interesting recent trends in business is the number of publicly held companies—MGM/UA, Avis, and Sotheby's come immediately to mind—which have either gone private or have attempted to go private. I suspect many major stockholders are coming to a conclusion I came to many years ago: It may just be too hard to try to run a company and keep the stockholders happy at the same time. That is the reason IMG will never go public.

American business decisions are often based on winning a popularity contest, on impressing certain people. And the people everyone is trying to impress work on Wall Street.

Impressing Wall Street has become the Great American Corporate Pastime. Long-term gains are sacrificed for short-term benefits. Bad corporate decisions are made because a company would rather look good than be good. Real profit is thrown away in order to pep up the next quarter artificially.

We would all be a lot better off if more companies tried to impress themselves rather than the people who work at the lower tip of Manhattan.

Know Your Competition

Several years ago I was playing doubles in Geneva, Switzerland, with Victor Pecci against Bjorn Borg and his amateur partner, Swiss banking and shipping magnate Bruce Rappaport. Bjorn and I were both at the net only a few feet away from each other when Rappaport hit a soft lob, which I could see was not going to clear my head. Borg was in a defenseless position, and for the briefest of split seconds I thought it would be unfair to hit the ball directly at him. I did anyway of course. I smashed the ball right at his midsection—and Borg promptly whistled it past my head for a winning point.

Never underestimate your competition. I think a competitive spirit is essential to both personal and corporate business success. And how you stack up against the competition is one of the best yardsticks for measuring that success.

But there is a major difference between competing in business and competing in sports. In both cases the idea is to win, to beat everyone else. But in business there is no end to the game. There are no insurmountable leads. The competition always has time to catch up.

Companies with the greatest market share often have a tendency to "sit on a lead." They will take solace in their numbers, become complacent, and lose their competitive edge. Business competition, I believe, is a constant, ongoing, active process of domination.

The better you know your competition—their strengths, their weaknesses, their habits, their tactics—the more you will be able to dominate them, or even take advantage of them.

In any sort of representative business, or in any business where you are paid on a percentage basis, if you aren't careful you can spend as much time representing the also-rans as you can the superstars. Many years ago, when sports clients who were in this questionable category approached us, we referred them to a particular competitor whose weaknesses we knew. While we could never be sure which of these players would develop into champions, we were 100 percent sure this firm would do a poor job representing them. Once the winners emerged from the pack we could go after them with absolute certainty that we could sign them up.

Avoid Ego Diversification

We have had sports clients who, because of their exceptional success in a very narrow field, automatically presume that they can conquer the world in any other field as well: tennis players who decide to be exhibition promoters; golfers who decide to be real estate developers; Olympic champions who decide to be publishers and run magazines. Many athletes, once they retire, want to run camps and schools, not recognizing the administrative skills and specialized expertise this requires.

We generally try to stop them from getting into these areas without first acquiring that necessary expertise. But the egos of leading sports personalities, like the egos of many successful business people, will not listen to reason.

A lot of established companies, as they feel the need to grow and expand, begin to buy companies that they don't have any business being in. At some level they know that they lack the expertise, the real understanding of how the business works, but their egos won't let them admit this to themselves. The American corporate landscape is littered with the bodies of these egotistical acquisitions.

Don't Sue the Bastards

Someone told me that last year IBM paid $12 million in legal fees to a single law firm.

I graduated from Yale Law School and practiced law with the firm of Arter & Hadden of Cleveland, Ohio, which is Cleveland's oldest and one of its most prestigious law firms. I am still a partner of the firm, yet I must say that the entire judicial system of the United States leaves me cold.

Fights between law firms on behalf of clients are often mere vehicles for firms to charge time and earn money. I feel that if you can put the two parties in most legal disputes in a room by themselves—even two years into the legal dispute—the matter will get resolved, certainly more cheaply, and probably a lot more equitably.

We have been fairly lucky with lawsuits in our business in the sense that we have not had that many. Since so many of us were trained as lawyers, I think we realize all the pitfalls and expenses that can be incurred when you start legal proceedings.

In other parts of the world the losers in lawsuits pay the winner's legal fees in addition to court costs and the judgments. To me this is a far better system. It discourages frivolous lawsuits and the knee-jerk business reaction of "see you in court."

The Japanese seem to work things out among themselves better than anyone. While many people have pointed out that there are no business schools in Japan, no one seems to have noticed that there are also very few law firms in Japan.

We were once sued, along with our client Bjorn Borg, by Lamar Hunt, who has a battery of lawyers working for him. I decided that it was foolish from a business standpoint for Lamar Hunt to be suing Bjorn Borg when he was trying at the same time to run the World Championship Tennis tour and obviously wanted Borg to play in some of his tournaments. I therefore went to Dallas and saw Lamar personally. We sat down in a room together and in one meeting settled the suit. Had this been left up to the lawyers we would still be in court, and hundreds and thousands of dollars would have gone down the drain.

13 | Getting Things Done

I F EXECUTIVES WERE ASKED to list their greatest frustrations, I suspect that not having enough time would be very near the top of the list. The constant flow of business provides an equally constant flow of interruptions which keep people from spending their time the way they had planned to. Something always comes up, and they find themselves further behind at the end of the day than when they began.

The solutions to these problems are a lot simpler than people are often willing to admit. It is mostly a matter of controlling your business day rather than having it control you, of forcing activities into the time available rather than trying to expand the time to accommodate the activities.

But many people fear that if they don't seem out of control they aren't going to seem busy enough or important enough. They really don't *want* to manage their time well.

Once you really believe that controlling your time is not only more productive but more pleasant, then the rest is fairly easy.

Time Management

The one thing that people who know me best attribute to me the most is an ability to manage my time efficiently.

I begin by viewing a week as 168 hours, and I schedule time for relaxation and rest as well as work. I force myself to have time to relax, be it to play tennis, to read the morning paper, to take a nap in the office, or simply to do nothing—to free my mind from any sort of work-oriented thoughts or decisions. To make sure I have this time I program these nonwork activities into my schedule. If I know, for instance, that my first time commitment is at 7 AM, I would rather get up at 5 AM and spend an hour reading, relaxing, and exercising than get up at 6 AM and have to rush to my first appointment without having time to myself. My schedule that day would therefore begin at 5 AM.

I hate leaving unfinished business or having anything hanging over my head, and I work with great intensity to obtain moments of empty space—a minute, an hour, or a weekend—in which to enjoy having nothing to do. These moments are the carrots at the end of my stick, and by programming them into my schedule I force myself to finish the business activities leading up to them within the time specifically allocated for them.

This has led to a kind of heightened state of time consciousness. I always perceive any business activity or commitment as a function of the time I have allotted for it. I also play a kind of game with myself. If a meeting is starting in one hour and I have decided there are ten things I want to accomplish before that meeting begins, I will do whatever is necessary to fit all ten things into that hour. It may mean making a phone call a lot shorter than I would have liked, or dashing off a note rather than a letter, but by challenging myself this way, by fitting activities into smaller and smaller time segments, I have over the years developed an almost minute-by-minute awareness of how I am spending my time.

I pretty well know how long it takes me to do everything, and I pretty well know the quickest way to do everything, from how fast or slow certain restaurants are and in which ones you therefore have to order immediately to the fastest elevators in certain buildings. When arriving at airports, for instance, I will often have people meet me at the departure ramp, which is almost never as crowded as the arrival area and therefore much quicker.

In short, I try to be very precise about everything that by its nature is imprecise. My mind is a catalogue of "quick cuts" which allow me to reduce the time-wasting vagueness of certain activities or to avoid them altogether.

When traveling internationally, for instance, I know which carriers, such as Qantas to Australia and Cathay Pacific to Asia, put priority tags on first-class luggage. I know that Concorde baggage clearance is quick, that early morning arrivals in London for Americans and in Honolulu from Asia and Australia are disasters, and that international arrivals into LAX are disasters at almost any time. I have found that I am even something of an expert on traffic flow and rush hours in the major cities of the world.

It is simply a matter of using this information to my time-saving advantage, or making certain prearrangements based on this information. For instance, I usually travel light and carry on everything. But to do this constantly I maintain a complete wardrobe in each of my five principal residences and a partial wardrobe at those offices where I don't have a separate residence. And if I know I will need something in Paris I will send it directly there rather than carry it with me first to New York and then to London.

I have used some international travel examples here because they are so "unmanageable" by nature. But I try to take this same approach to every aspect of my business. By knowing how long it will take me to do something and by knowing the quickest way to get it done, I can take control over things that may not seem all that controllable.

As a general rule for getting things done the quickest, *do the things that everyone else has to do at the times when everyone else isn't doing them.* I leave so early in the morning that getting to work is never a problem. But I've heard others complain about rush hour traffic, then admit that if they'd left twenty minutes earlier it could have been avoided. The answer seems so obvious, and yet so many people have difficulty making a simple twenty-minute adjustment in their schedule. They'd rather be miserable for an hour on the freeway.

I've seen employees get a paycheck on Friday, try to cash it between twelve and three that afternoon, then *complain* because the lines were so long! I have also seen some of our own executives who are flying out of New York schedule a departure time that will compete with everyone else who is trying to get home. Ninety percent of wasting time and standing in line can be eliminated with a little preplanning and some common sense.

An Organization System

The whole solution to mastering time is to do the things *you* planned on doing *when* you planned on doing them and for *no longer* than you planned on doing them. This demands that you work from some overall organizational system.

I operate both my life and my time from a series of yellow legal pads, with one sheet devoted to each day and a vertical line drawn down the middle. Things to do go on the right side of the vertical line, people to call go on the left side. I keep this pad in about fifty-day segments, and at the end I have several pages for calls and activities which are not going to be done during this fifty-day time frame but at some point in the future.

When I ask someone when he would like me to call, and he says next Wednesday at about 10:30, I will put that person's name and phone number about a third of the way down the left-hand side of the page marked for next Wednesday. Late afternoon and evening calls and activities occupy the bottom third of the page, and early morning activities the top third of the page. I review this pad periodically during the day to see how I am doing. If I'm getting behind, I will rarely eliminate anything, but I will pick up the pace.

I also keep a separate pad with pages marked for different parts of the world. If someone says to me, "Get in touch with so-and-so when you're in Melbourne," or if something comes up that I must handle personally in Tokyo, I will make a notation on the relevant page.

In addition to my yellow pads, I always have a stack of three-by-five cards in any coat pocket. Some of them are marked with the names of employees or business associates with whom I am in regular contact. If I think of something in relation to one of these people, I jot it down on the appropriate card. The next time I speak to that person I will have everything I want to talk about at my fingertips.

I also carry a stack of blank cards that I fill up with miscellaneous notes during the day, and at the end of the day I transfer that information to the appropriate page of the appropriate yellow pad.

I write down everything I intend to do, and once I have written it down I forget about it. I know it will turn up at the appropriate time and place on the appropriate day.

Obviously, how you choose to organize your work life is the most personal of all aspects of time management. I know people who use a pocket calendar and a notebook the same way I use yellow pads and note cards. I have worked with people who seldom organize more than one week in advance. And I have seen people work quite efficiently simply from a "to do" list unrelated to time itself.

Yet I have never known a successful person in business who didn't operate from some personal organizational system.

There are two points about the way I organize myself which have an almost universal application.

First, write it down. Write it down anywhere, on your

shirtsleeves if necessary, but write it down. This allows you to free your mind for other things. But more important, *it means you are going to do it*. Writing something down is a commitment. Once you have performed this physical act, you have provided the momentum for getting something done. The agony of carrying over an item and the ecstasy that comes with crossing it off will provide further incentive.

Second, *organize for the next day at the end of the previous day*. This is what gives me peace of mind at night, a feeling that I am on top of things, and a real excitement about coming into work the next morning. Simply by arranging the next day—defining on paper what I want to accomplish—I feel that I have a head start.

I do the same thing periodically over longer time spans: weekly, monthly, bimonthly, semiannually, annually, and biannually, on up to some general things I want to accomplish over the next five years.

Stick to Your Schedule

An itinerary or schedule is worthless if you don't stick to it.

A large part of sticking to your schedule is an awareness that it is very rare that something is so important or a crisis is so imminent that it has to be attended to immediately. Treat interruptions or anything else that just comes up as you would any other time commitment. Don't respond immediately, but program time for dealing with these situations into your future schedule—that afternoon, tomorrow, or next week—wherever you have a space to fit them in or can make the space to fit them in.

The other major aspect of sticking to your schedule is allocating the appropriate amount of time to the activities that will be filling it up.

It is probably worse to allocate too little time than it is to allocate too much. This puts you in a position of always having to catch up, which backs up through your schedule and usually gets worse as the day wears on.

I think most people can predict with reasonable accuracy how long their usual business activities will take them, but they will often deceive themselves.

To manage time well, you have to *believe in your own knowledge*. If you know a weekly meeting takes thirty minutes, don't convince yourself that today it will only take fifteen minutes, simply because today you have more to do. If you have to be somewhere in ten minutes and you have ten minutes to get there, don't make one more phone call simply because you want to get it out of the way. People who manage their time badly seem to want to be unrealistic and go out of their way to create out-of-control situations.

Allocate Personalities

Since most of the business day is spent dealing with people, you have to factor in their styles and personalities when budgeting your time. I have certain people working for me with whom I can cover twenty-five subjects in a fifteen-minute phone call. I have others with whom that would take all week, who have a need to make even the simplest statements the beginning of a drawn-out dialogue. This is the nature of certain people, and I'm not going to be able to change it. It's much wiser simply to budget more time for them or to discuss fewer subjects.

You should obviously have a pretty good idea of the number and complexity of the subjects to be discussed before meeting with anyone, but how long each will take also depends on two human factors: how quickly the other person gets and/or gets to the point; and his or her personal style of doing business.

When dealing with Bob Anderson, chairman of Rockwell, for instance, I know he will usually get the point before I even finish my sentence. I also know that finishing the sentence anyway just for the sake of finishing it will be a waste of his time.

On the other hand, Roone Arledge, the exceptionally capable head of the ABC network's news and sports division, has a style of doing business that is totally different. We have had several lunch meetings which meandered on through the afternoon. On one occasion the restaurant's dinner patrons began arriving while we were still having brandy and coffee.

This is Roone Arledge's style, which is very effective for him, and therefore, when I am dealing with him, the most effective for me. I will simply allocate the appropriate amount of time for lunch on those particular days. Rather than make myself anxious by scheduling a host of other afternoon commitments, I will most likely leave the rest of the day blank.

Learn everything about the people you are dealing with, including the way they like to do business and their own time management habits. I know the people who will invariably be twenty or thirty minutes late for a meeting, and I will plan on that. I will allocate meetings with them later on my schedule than they have on theirs and use the time differential to get several things accomplished. This is much more productive than getting irritated and hoping that they show up on time for a change.

Phone Calls

Phone calls and meetings take up most of my day and, I imagine, the better part of most executives' days. If you can get these two business activities under control, everything else will fall in place.

I seldom accept any phone call. It is usually an interruption, and I would rather deal with it in my own time and when I can focus my attention on the call rather than on what I am already doing. Initiating a phone call also gives me more control and time to plan what I want to say.

But I return every phone call, with two exceptions: if I simply don't want to talk to the caller; or if the call is better handled by someone else in our organization (in which case I make sure that the appropriate person gets back to the caller).

Returning every phone call is more a matter of personal style than of time management, but it works for me because I don't have to spend a lot of time keeping track of whom I haven't called or feeling guilty about it.

Pause to Anticipate

I wasn't even aware that I did this, but someone pointed it out to me. Whenever my secretary buzzes to tell me the other party is on the line, I put my hand on the receiver and pause a moment before actually picking it up. What I am doing is taking a few final seconds to anticipate: What do I want to accomplish and what's the quickest way to accomplish it?

I heard this line once: "If you don't know where you're going you'll end up somewhere else." There's probably no greater truism about talking on the phone. If you're not crystal clear in your own mind about what you want to accomplish, you probably won't end up accomplishing it.

Get to the Point

Though I am pretty good at allocating my time, in order to stick to my schedule I still often find myself forcing the end of phone calls.

I am a great believer that it is not difficult to get to the point or to end a phone call quickly, and yet I see many people who have trouble doing this. Typically people on the telephone will take five times longer than necessary to say what has to be said. They equate ending a telephone call with being impolite or insensitive.

If I want to end a call and I know the person well, I just tell him that I have to go or that I will get back to him later. If I don't know him well, I might say something like, "There are three or four people waiting outside for a meeting which should have started five minutes ago," or "I have got a call coming in from Switzerland on the other line that I have been trying to get all day."

I also like to get to the point of the phone call first, *then* engage in any small talk as time may allow. Most people do the opposite. They chat for five minutes before getting around to the purpose of their call. Sometimes this may be appropriate, but far more often than not, in addition to wasting your own time, you may be wasting the time of the person you called. Even worse, he may have to take another call, and you will hang up without having said the one thing you called to say.

Finally, I can pretty well estimate how long it will take me to make all my phone calls on a particular day. If I have promised to return a call at a specific time I will make that call very close to when I said I would. For all remaining calls, I will allocate a time period—usually thirty to ninety minutes—and set that time aside.

I will then list the phone calls in the order I want to make them, and I will put at the end those calls which *I can easily shorten* if pressed for time. Listing calls in this manner—by the latitude I have for shortening them—almost always allows me to stick to my allocated time frame.

This also means that I usually save most of my staff and internal calls for last, when, if necessary, I can be more abrupt.

How to Shorten the Long Maybe

Every phone call should accomplish something. If you can't get a definite response out of someone, get the outside date when he will have one. If you can't get this out of him either, get the outside date when he will be able to give you an outside date. If you can't even get this, forget it. Any further pursuit is almost certainly going to be a waste of your time, and just in knowing this you've already accomplished a great deal.

How to Avoid Phone Tag

Sometimes the most you can accomplish is to find out when you will actually be able to speak to the other party. A lot of people waste a lot of time going back and forth just trying to reach one another.

It should rarely take more than two phone calls to reach anyone, as long as you initiate both calls. When you can't reach the other party the first time, don't ask him or her to return your call. Find out when he will be available, then volunteer to call back again.

I have often asked the secretary of the person I am trying to reach when that person might be able to return my call. Once I have extracted a specific date and time, I will then say that I will call back at that time. If you can't get this kind of information, establish a very narrow time window for calling again: "Please tell Mr. So-and-So that I will try to reach him this afternoon between 2:45 and 3:00 PM." People will schedule commitments around your call just so they will be available.

If it takes more than two phone calls to reach someone, it is probably not a logistical problem. It is more likely a case of the other person not wanting to talk to you.

How to Make Them Take Your Call

Tell them something they want to hear or something they will be afraid not to hear.

I once received a call from someone I didn't know, and the message was, "I've got some great news." It turned out to be one of those telephone solicitations, but at least I did return the call.

Recently I called the chairman of a major airline, whom I did not know very well, about a sports promotion we were packaging. Since I knew none of the airlines has any money these days and since we can always use airline travel credits, I said to his secretary, "Please tell Mr. So-and-So that I have an idea I'd like to discuss with him, and if he really likes it, it won't cost him any money." He took the call.

If you and the other party have a mutual acquaintance, *and you know their relationship is a good one,* the use of this name will almost always get you through. If the call is really important, you can make an acquaintance just for that purpose. I have known people who, when trying to reach a specific individual within another company, will first call the company's president and confirm with his secretary that this individual is indeed the person to whom they should be speaking. When they make the call they begin by saying that Mr. So-and-So's office suggested that they should be talking to this particular person.

Silence Means Consent

A phone call doesn't have to be a two-way communication. If you are just imparting information rather than exchanging or discussing it, leave a detailed message and don't call back. If the party has any questions he'll get back to you.

If you are calling for a simple answer to a question, to confirm something, or to get the other party's support or agreement, couch the call in such a way that silence means consent. "Please have Mr. So-and-So call me back only if he disagrees."

I have known some very effective salesmen who use this to set up appointments and who get in to see people they don't even know or who otherwise wouldn't see them: "Write on Mr. So-and-So's calendar that I will stop by at 10:30 next Wednesday. If this is inconvenient, please have him call me."

Who Gets on First?

Some executives are really hung up over power protocol when it comes to talking on the phone. They refuse to punch the buttons themselves and spend a lot of time making sure they are never on the phone first. Again, you have to know the personalities of the people with whom you are dealing.

I know the people who think that I am trying to one-up them in some way if I am not already on the phone when they pick up. When I call these people I always make sure I'm on the phone first.

I know the people who resent having their secretaries take information for them or who always prefer to set up their own appointments. And I know the people who like to answer the phone themselves, and I make sure I always deal with these people myself. I know the people I can interrupt and the people who would find this the ultimate business insult.

There are some executives who think that secretaries should only talk to other secretaries and would find it distressing if I personally set up an appointment through their secretary rather than having one of my secretaries do it for me.

Know the characters of the people you are dealing with and observe their phone protocol, not your own—even if theirs is sometimes a bit silly.

Internal Meetings

Staff and internal meetings are the bane of corporate life. They are essential to communication and decision making, yet most of them go nowhere, accomplish nothing, and waste everyone's time. Since they can't be eliminated, minimize their number, their frequency, and their length.

Who Are These People and What Are They Doing in My Meeting?

Rule: A meeting's productivity is inversely proportionate to the number of people attending it. First corollary: Beyond four or five attendees, productivity decreases exponentially. Second corollary: The longer a meeting has been in existence, the bigger it becomes.

The vast majority of internal meetings are attended by more people than need to be there. This can be attributed to two realities of corporate life.

First, every company has its quota of executives who judge the value of what they have to say by the number of people who are forced to listen to them. For these executives an important meeting is one in which there aren't enough chairs to go around.

Second, there is the "left-out factor." Meetings have a way of becoming part of the corporate merit system, and people begin to judge their importance to the company by the number and nature of the meetings they are asked to attend. Assigning a meeting a regular time slot or giving it a name guarantees the left-out factor will become even greater.

We once had a small informal committee which met infrequently and irregularly for the purpose of making decisions in a very narrow area. But over the years both its size and purpose grew until it was no longer conducive to decision making and became strictly informational. Still, everyone wanted to attend. Finally I took the position that this committee should meet once a year, that everyone who wanted to could attend, and that its purpose would no longer be decision making *or* informational but strictly to make everyone feel good. That lent some perspective, and we were able to go back once again to a small gathering.

Meetings, like corporate policies, should be reviewed regularly—for their frequency, their necessity, and their size. People who might otherwise wish to attend may be just as content to receive the minutes. Others might actually be pleased *not* to attend and would like nothing better than to have their time back for more productive purposes.

I have occasionally set arbitrary guidelines to determine who qualifies to attend our most "popular" meetings—the guidelines determined by whom I did and did not want to be there. What this may lack in fairness is more than made up for in lack of argument.

Fold in Meetings

Both the frequency and purposes of most regularly scheduled meetings can be significantly altered without any loss of effectiveness.

The start-up time alone of meetings—the time it takes for everyone to show up, get settled in, and get rolling—is a big drain on corporate man-hours. Very often a one-hour monthly meeting can be more productive than two forty-five-minute biweekly ones. Any meeting that is held more than once a month should be scrutinized very carefully.

Many meetings have parallel or overlapping functions which can easily be folded into one another or combined.

The irony of meetings is that they follow a reverse Parkinson's law: The number of subjects to be discussed contracts to accommodate the time available. Meetings that are folded in or combined in their purpose or frequency are far more productive.

While meetings are essential to the decision-making process, they are not the best forum for decision making, and if more than four or five people are in attendance, decision making is probably next to impossible.

Decision making by committee is neither efficient nor effective, and the decisions that result are usually not the best ones. It is also difficult to cede accountability to a committee. Further, the quickest way for a meeting to get out of hand is to announce that a decision must be reached before it ends.

Meetings which are more than just informational should be used to let people air their views—to *help* the ultimate decision maker decide. But it is best for the decision itself to come later. This eliminates further discussion, minimizes confrontation, discourages public influence peddling, and lends clarity to the decision itself.

How to Run a Meeting

The time a meeting is to begin and the *time it is to end* should be established as early as possible, committed to paper (thus encouraging punctuality), and distributed by name to every attendee. Meetings that begin at an oddball time—10:15 as opposed to 10:30—are also generally attended with greater punctuality.

If several subjects are to be discussed, an agenda should be distributed and/or given to each attendee as he or she arrives. This is less to inform than to move the meeting along. If everyone knows when the meeting is to end and can see the number of subjects still to be covered, it will be easier to cut off discussion on one subject and move on to the next.

If I am chairing, I will generally place the shorter informational subjects at the beginning of a meeting and save the longer subjects or discussion points for the end.

On these longer, more discussion-oriented subjects I will first summarize the topic and all the sides to the issue in order to eliminate a lot of back-and-forth.

Meet in Hallways

I would like to find the guy who first said, "There is no such thing as a stupid question," and force him to sit through the monthly meeting cycle of any major corporation. A "stupid question" is any that could be asked just as easily before or after the meeting and enlightens no one but the person asking it.

I would venture that half the scheduled meetings in the average American company could be done away with entirely and never missed. Scheduling a meeting is often the automatic response to dealing with those subjects which are slightly too complex to handle internally over the telephone. "Meeting in hallways"—that is, any short, informal gathering of three or four people to exchange information or to get a quick consensus—is a better, more efficient alternative.

People will also be less upset about not being "invited."

External Meetings

One obviously has greater control and more authority over the length of an internal meeting than over an external one. Yet even when meeting with someone outside the company—at his office or mine—I have become fairly adept at forcing the meeting's length into the time I have allocated for it.

To do this successfully one must establish immediately and as the first order of business—either by setting the agenda or by coming right out and saying it—the amount of time one has available. Most people will appreciate this. It gives them a better idea of how much time they should allocate to each subject.

Again, I contend that the initial moments of a meeting—

from exchanging greetings to getting down to business—
are more crucial to its content and critical to its outcome
than anything that is likely to follow. I use this time to set
the agenda, the tone, and the atmosphere and to make
certain desired impressions. For this reason I eliminate all
extraneous activity from the beginning of a meeting. I will
not have anyone shown into my office until I am off the
phone or have finished shuffling papers and can devote my
total attention to the person I am meeting with. I will rarely
allow any phone call or business matter to interrupt the
flow of these initial moments. I will get coffee or drink
orders out of the way, *and served,* before commencing any
business dialogue. If I can control these first few minutes I
will not only determine the meeting's length but almost
everything else about it as well.

If it's time to end a meeting and the other person doesn't
seem to want to, there are all sorts of things you can say or
body language you can use. (On occasion I've even picked
up the phone receiver and cradled it in my hand.) You just
have to be willing to say or use them.

Many times a meeting between two parties who don't
know each other very well will drag on and on because
each is waiting for the other to end it. The slightest hint
will usually bring these meetings to a conclusion.

Where It's Best to Go Slow

Of course, one must also recognize (as in the case of a
Roone Arledge) the people for whom any appearance of
concern with time can work against your main purposes.
Most of our executives prefer to move quickly, jump from
deal to deal, leap into a problem or a situation, solve it or
get it done, and move on to the next one. It is absolutely
essential to know who among the people you deal with is
rubbed the wrong way by this hyperactive approach.

Generally speaking, the Japanese consider the desire to

end a meeting shortly after it begins a breach of etiquette and a break with their own customs and culture. If you try to get from A to B too quickly you may not get there at all.

In our business the same thing is true in dealing with the heads of sports federations. These are usually unpaid positions, and the people who take them on do so not because they must but because they want to: It is their hobby. When you try to make a meeting with them as short as possible or force them to the point rather than let them talk around, over, and under it, you are often cutting your own throat.

I once dealt with a British sports official who was so slow to do anything he probably, in the words of our business associate, "screwed his shoes on in the morning." We would have lunch together, and it would often take me literally three hours to get him onto the first point.

He also never wanted a meeting to end, and I finally got to the point where when I wanted to indicate that I had to leave I would take off my watch and put it on the table in front of us. Yet he was so oblivious to the time concerns of others I was sure he didn't even notice. But he did. One day he mentioned to our mutual business associate this peculiar habit I had of removing my watch during lunch and wondered if I hadn't lost a lot of watches that way.

Restaurant Meetings

Breakfast, lunch, and dinner meetings are an important part of my business day for, as I said, I prefer them to office meetings: They are automatically more intimate, more friendly, and less formal; they are more revealing about the person; the other person is more vulnerable and receptive.

I take great care to assure that the atmosphere of these meetings is not only relaxed but conducive to business. First, and for all the reasons mentioned above, I seldom have restaurant meetings with more than one person. (With two or more guests, the psychological dynamics become more variable and therefore more difficult to interpret or control.)

Second, particularly in New York, Paris, and London, where one is often seated nearer to the person at the next table than to the person one is meeting with, I never make reservations for less than three. This at least gets me out of sardine row.

Third, I will not turn to business until the meal has been ordered and the menus taken away. Since I believe the first minute or two are so important in establishing everything that is to follow, I find it disconcerting to have a waiter hovering over or around the table while I am trying to make my initial points.

Finally, while I have never been driven by the need to dine only at "power" restaurants (in fact, I often question the real power of those who must), I do believe in frequenting those which understand the business dining atmosphere: restaurants which take as much pain to assure peace, quiet, and tranquillity as they do to prepare their specials of the day.

Know Your Own Work Habits

I have learned over the years how to arrange my schedule to accommodate my work habits. The early morning is my best time for thinking and for making phone calls to the different parts of the world where business days have already begun. I will usually get up two to three hours before my first actual time commitment to do everything from push-ups to business reading to overseas phone calls. I also tend to have a lot of early morning meetings. Most of our staff meetings start at 7:00 or 7:30, and more often than not I will have two breakfast meetings before arriving at the office. My first office activity of the day is almost always dictation, when my mind is clearest.

By noon I usually have a pretty good leg up on the day, and my afternoons are slightly less frenetic. I will save those appointments and activities for last which are most likely to be open-ended or where I can be the most relaxed. About half my evenings involve some business-related activity. The others are set aside as rewards. I also use travel time for rest and relaxation as much as for getting from one place to the next.

I have found that most people function better in the earlier part of the day and seem to drag a bit right after lunch. But I'm sure there are others who are just the opposite, who gain momentum and pick up speed as the day goes on. What's important is that you know your own time clock and plan your day accordingly.

Once you have organized your work day in a way that is best for you, *stick to it.* I will, for instance, occasionally dictate in a limousine on the way to the airport, but otherwise I dictate in the morning, period. In over twenty years I can count on my fingers the times when a letter or memo was so important it couldn't wait until the next morning.

For me, getting the most out of my abilities is directly proportionate to getting the most out of my time. I take an aggressive attitude toward time, and I seek to control it rather than have it control me.

Nevertheless, one of the very simple realities of effective personal time management may be that *the forty-hour work week is only for unions.* I've never met a successful businessman who didn't put in considerably more than forty hours a week. In fact, the people I know who spend the most hours are also the people who make the best use of these hours. The two often seem to go hand in hand.

By organizing myself in a way that fits my personal work habits, by planning out my leisure time as well as my work time, and by writing everything down, I am able to free my mind totally from work-related thoughts when I am not working and focus totally on work when I am. This allows me not to carry my problems to bed with me at night. I sleep like a log.

Learn to Say No Even When It Hurts

The best instant time saver I know of is to say no. People have a hard time doing this even when it is the obvious response. They are afraid they may offend someone, they may be hedging their bets, or they may simply not want to make a decision at that particular moment.

It is very easy to say no without being impolite. A no expressed with reluctance or regret, or with a believable excuse ("If I wasn't so pressed for time ..." "If I had known about this six months ago ...") can be just as final and definitive as "I'm not interested."

The bigger problem is a reluctance to be final, a feeling that there is a chance, however remote, that one may be missing an opportunity. There have been many occasions when I have found myself in this situation and I have forced myself to say no even when it hurt.

Just recently we were approached about packaging a major sports event which was already financed. Even though I knew we could probably make it work, I felt the cost in time and manpower was too great and declined. Every opportunity has to be considered in the context of other commitments, and occasionally you are going to miss out on one. But if you try to sniff out every opportunity until you are 100 percent certain one way or the other, you may find yourself bringing an entire company to its knees.

By far the biggest problem people have with saying no is that they convince themselves that by buying time they are actually saving time. If you are feeling overwhelmed or harassed, it is much easier to say, "Let me think about it," or "Let me get back to you," than it is to deal with it and get it out of the way. This is particularly tempting when you already know the answer is going to be a negative one.

Obviously these situations don't just go away, and by not taking five minutes to deal with it at the moment you invariably end up spending a lot more time with it in the future.

I have been on the receiving end of many no's and I actually prefer an instant negative response to an excessively long, drawn-out maybe. Usually these end up wasting my time and come to the same conclusion anyway.

A no is often better for everyone. It saves time on both sides, and it will give you a sense of satisfaction. The realization that you won't have to deal with it again can make you feel like you've really accomplished something.

Decision Making

Someone once told me that when the Ford Motor Company interviews a managerial-level applicant they note whether the potential employee puts salt and pepper on his food before he tastes it, the theory being that such a person is likely to make a decision before knowing all the facts.

I hope this isn't true, first because I don't think it has anything to do with decision making—I know some excellent decision makers who happen to like their food very spicy—and second because one of the biggest problems people have with decision making is a desire to know *too many* facts, their theory being that if you have enough facts the decision will make itself.

The people I respect the most in business are all instant decision makers. They don't need to know every "knowable" fact first. They accept that they are going to make their share of wrong decisions and are self-confident enough to know that most of the time they are going to make the right one.

A reputation as a good decision maker is usually based as much on how quickly and definitely that person decides as it is on the results.

The Seat-of-the-Pants Factor

Some companies, asked the simplest question, always respond with the same non-answer: "I think we've got some data on that."

Decison making is more an intuitive process than an analytical one, and no number of market studies, focus groups, or research reports is going to change that fact. The danger is that the more data people have to chew upon, the more likely they are to underestimate the importance of intuition—the seat-of-the-pants factor.

In sales, as previously noted, good or correct timing is often a matter of converting sensory perception into conscious action. Decision making is exactly the same process, only the flow is reversed. It is taking analytical data, facts and figures, and converting them into sensory perceptions. If you eliminate the need to "feel" a decision, you won't make very good decisions or you won't make them at all.

I once heard a story of a Columbia University scientist who had received a grant to study how sound vibrations might be used to exterminate insects. In one experiment, he trained a roach to leap over a pencil at the command of "Jump!" But during the course of the experiment the roach became trapped in a drawer and in an effort to extricate itself lost some of its legs.

The scientist noted that, after the accident, whenever he yelled "Jump!" the roach just sat there. In a report on his findings, he concluded, "The roach was so traumatized by the loss of its legs it went deaf."

Facts are a decision maker's tools, but (1) they won't take the place of intuition, (2) they won't make the decision for you, and (3) they are only as useful as your ability to interpret them.

Some people ignore the facts altogether ("Don't clutter up my mind with a bunch of details"), but a far greater number use them to justify convenient or already established positions rather than the one the facts actually support. It is obviously difficult to make good decisions based on self-assuring, self-justifying, or self-serving bad conclusions.

Look Around the Fringes

The best use of facts—marketing data, surveys, reports, what people are telling you—is not their literal interpretation but what they may indicate. A stop sign tells you to stop, but what it indicates is conflicting traffic patterns and certain consequences if you ignore it.

Look around the fringes. What do the facts indicate about trends, biases, conflicts, opportunities?

One kind of decision maker will say, "We shouldn't do this because three other people tried it and failed," but a good decision maker will find out what all three did similarly and what all three failed to do similarly before reaching the same conclusion.

Look Beyond the Fringes

The most useful decision-making information may lie beyond the facts. Don't be bound only by what you already know.

As successful as we have been in establishing an income base for our sports clients after they retire, there is an inevitable drop-off in income once they are no longer competing actively. Realistically, this hurts us corporately more than it does the athlete personally. A Bjorn Borg, for instance, who decides to retire, can still live as nicely on $1 million and royalties as he can on the $5 million he was making annually as an active tennis professional. But as a company which maintains a steady overhead, the loss of 80 percent of our commission income can be significant. It puts a constant pressure on us always to be looking for the "next Borg," even when there isn't one out there.

In grappling with this problem several years ago I came to the conclusion that this was the particular nature of our business and had to be factored in just like anything else. But in coming to this conclusion my mind was no longer constricted by the obvious facts, and a totally different solution, outside the facts, occurred to me. The answer was to represent a mix of both sports personalities and sports entities. That led to the creation and licensing of a Wimbledon logo, one of our most successful licensing programs to date and certainly one of the steadiest. Wimbledon does not have to win tournaments to maintain visibility, and it won't retire. It has given us a steady, predictable source of income to balance the more volatile areas of athlete representation.

Sound corporate decision making is a constant process of staying current, of perceiving how new information can alter old decisions, of anticipating the future.

Elephantine Decision Making

A circus keeps a baby elephant from running away by chaining it to a stake. When the animal pulls at the chain the cuff chafes its leg, and the baby elephant concludes that to avoid pain it best stay put.

But when the elephant grows up, the circus still chains it to the same small stake. The mature elephant could now pull the stake out of the ground like a toothpick, but the elephant remembers the pain and is too dumb to use the new set of facts—how circumstances have changed. The tiny stake keeps a two-ton elephant at bay just as effectively as it did the baby.

Many executives are too dependent on old facts, on outmoded conventions, or are still basing decisions on what worked twenty years ago. This is elephantine decision making.

Go with First Impressions, But . . .

I almost always go with first impressions, but I let them settle in for a period of time. Decisions are—and should be—partly emotional, but it is helpful to keep your options open until the cold harsh light of day has had a chance to shine on them: Are there any obvious considerations that haven't been considered? If none occurs to me in the first twenty-four hours, this means they will probably never occur to me—or that by the time they do it will be too late anyway.

Good Decisions Are Self-fulfilling

If you immediately start to second-guess a decision you have made it will most likely prove a bad one, not because it was the wrong decision but because you have undermined its chance for success.

A lot of questionable decisions have worked because the people who made them were determined to make them work, and a lot of good decisions have failed because the people who made them never got over their doubts.

When I first decided we were going to create and market a Wimbledon logo, I met all sorts of resistance from people in our company who would be involved in the effort. First, Wimbledon had been around for almost a century, and if this was such a good idea why hadn't someone else done it? Second, there was much supporting evidence that people would identify with a Borg or a Palmer or a fashion designer but none that they would wear the name of a tennis tournament on their shirt. Finally, and most damagingly, we were starting in the hole. Over twenty-five companies worldwide were already using the name *Wimbledon* generically on their products. Our legal department doubted we could even clean up the market, much less create one.

But I believed that a Wimbledon logo should work and that we were the ones to make it work. Had I been less convinced of this, or had I simply been looking for signs to tell me I was wrong, I'm sure Wimbledon would have remained a generic name, available to anyone who cared to use it.

Flip a Coin

Many times you have actually made a decision before you realize it—and even though you are still trying to come to grips with it.

Instead of laboring over the pros and cons, try this: Flip a coin. Heads you do it; tails you don't. Now how do you *feel* about the result? You may be surprised to find that your emotional reaction settles the issue for you—confirms what you unconsciously know.

Office Communication

I believe that how quickly things get done in an office, how quickly information gets exchanged, is more a matter of style than of systems.

As I have said, I prefer quick, informal exchanges of information to the more formal, and hence more time-consuming, atmosphere of meetings. I prefer visiting other people's offices rather than having them come to mine (it is a lot easier to leave someone else's office than it is to get someone else out of mine). I prefer catching someone in the hallway or asking him something over the telephone to arranging formal appointments which can take a minimum of five minutes to get twenty seconds' worth of information. In general I find that I pick up 90 percent of the pertinent information I need in these quick, informal encounters.

I am much more likely to ask our executives for a "one-liner" or "bulletin" on a particular subject than I am for a formal report. When I am leaving after visiting one of our offices, I will often set aside the final ten or fifteen minutes of the trip for this purpose. I will drop in on several people on my way out either to give them a one-liner or ask for one. I find this keeps me more current with various situations around the world than almost anything else I do.

These quick, informal exchanges have a tendency to flow down through the organization as a style of communicating. Employees often adopt the mannerisms and habits of their managers, and one of the most adoptable of these mannerisms is the way information gets exchanged. If a manager is good at exchanging information quickly, most of the people who work for him will also be good at it. If his style is ponderous or if he tends to restate the obvious or take more time than necessary to say what needs to be said, his whole department will invariably be this way.

A manager's personal style—how good he or she is at exchanging information—contributes more to a department's efficiency than the results of any structured or organizational brilliance.

To Write or Not to Write

If there is a reason to write—to record for future reference, to confirm an understanding, to get down a complex set of facts or numbers—then write. Even to cover yourself or to state your position because you suspect it may be questioned are valid reasons. But if there are no special reasons, ask yourself if verbal communication would not be better, simpler, and more efficient.

The most important thing to remember about written communication is that it creates more work than simply your time to write it and someone else's to read it.

Bob Anderson, chairman of Rockwell International, once told me that if an outside director has something to say to him he almost always prefers to hear it verbally. If the communication is written, then all kinds of possibilities loom and have to be considered. How should it be responded to? What was the sender really trying to say? Are there legal or SEC implications? Is this a recommendation—or a threat?

The same thing applies to most written communication between departments and executives. Committing words to paper means that certain implications must be considered. It may also mean having to consider implications that are better left unconsidered.

A good rule of thumb may be to write only under the circumstances mentioned earlier.

There are a few simple obvious rules that should be followed for internal memoranda:

- Always begin with "To," "From," the date, and the subject.
- Get to the point. A one-line memo has more impact than a two-line memo, and so on. Don't circle around the thought or dramatically build to reach it. There are no literary prizes for the Great American Memo.
- Keep it simple. Memos should be used to pass on information, not to discuss it. If it's a complicated issue, some type of interactive communication—a face-to-face discussion or a phone call—is more appropriate. Position or opinion memos can often lead to memo wars.
- Hold off sending any sort of controversial memo for twenty-four hours. "Response memos" (the first salvo of memo wars) often fall into this category. One can come back to haunt you even several years after you sent it.
- File memos are helpful. They record details you might otherwise forget. The facts in file memos are given a lot more credibility than the exact same facts

recalled weeks, months, or years later. And file memos don't demand a response.

There is one final point I want to make about paperwork in general and memos in particular. I try to write memos which can be read once, then thrown away. But that is what I do with most of my incoming mail, whether it's written that way or not.

Next to crossing something off my list, nothing gives me greater pleasure than filing papers in my wastebasket, and I would estimate this is the fate of 95 percent of my incoming paperwork. Over the years there have been a number of occasions when I have thrown something away and later really wished I had not. But this, I believe, is a small price to pay for never having to see the rest of the paperwork again.

That reminds me of the story about Lew Wasserman and his famous midnight wastebasket forays at MCA. Perhaps the story is apocryphal, but I've heard it repeated often enough so that even if it isn't true it might as well be.

Wasserman would purportedly sweep through the MCA offices in the late evening and throw paperwork he found on anyone's desk into the wastebasket. The next day the offended executives would be told, "If you can't get it done before you leave, then it's not worth doing."

This was obviously Wasserman's way of making certain employees aware of how they were using their time and was not meant to be taken literally. Still, a number of people who have met with me late in the day have joked, "Mark, you must not be very busy. There isn't a single piece of paper on your desk."

Streamline Your Office

I believe the way an office looks—how neat and clean it is, how streamlined it is set up—can have a profound effect on how quickly things get done.

When you walk into an office that looks disorganized, you start to feel disorganized. On several occasions we have asked our office personnel to keep their desks clean—keeping papers in files if just to hide them—and to eat their lunch in the space provided for it rather than at their desks.

The frequent response to these requests is that we are being petty and nit-picking. Obviously, if I felt this were less important I wouldn't keep insisting on it. But to me the efficiency of an office is directly proportionate to how efficient it looks.

I have been in offices that seem to have been set up by the Keystone Kops—copying centers several floors away from the departments that use them most; typing pools set off as separate departments, often on the floor with billing and accounting and other indirect services; filing systems several offices removed from the offices they belong to.

These are usually fairly simple things to correct. Maybe if efficiency experts spent more time moving furniture and less time analyzing systems many companies would find they were getting a lot more done.

14 | For Entrepreneurs Only

O NE OF THE MOST dramatic cultural shifts over the last thirty years has been a redefinition of the Great American Dream. People are no longer content to work for two cars in the garage and a house in the right school district. Today the enjoyment of the job itself may be even more important than the enjoyment of its tangible rewards.

A lot of people are convinced that they will never achieve total job satisfaction by working for someone else. Given the choice of becoming chairman of their company or owner of their own small enterprise, they would opt for the latter. Starting a business has become the new Great American Dream.

As someone who started his own business, I can testify it is everything it is supposed to be. However, as John Mack Carter, editor-in-chief of *Good Housekeeping* magazine, once said to me, "Ninety-nine percent of the people in the world should be working for somebody." I tend to agree, which is why the chapter on starting your own business comes at the end of this book instead of at the beginning.

If everyone who has talked about starting a business actually went out and did it, the whole nation would be self-employed. But most people would rather fantasize about it than actually try to make it happen.

The first thing you have to do is examine your motives and, in doing so, determine whether you are a dreamer or in the 1 percent.

If you want to be in your own business because you are "sick and tired of being told what to do," because you want more "freedom," or because you are unappreciated or undervalued, forget it. These are not reasons for starting a business; these are reasons for running away from your present job. If you want to "make a lot of money," that's probably not a great reason either. That is a fine and worthwhile goal, but if it is your prime motivation it is not going to be enough to get you through the lean years.

Before starting our company I was a lawyer with a prestigious Cleveland firm, but I knew I didn't want to spend the rest of my life practicing corporate law. I loved negotiating contracts, not drafting them, and the security of the paycheck wasn't going to be enough to keep me at the firm. I was cautious and apprehensive, but I was more intimidated by the thought of wasting my time and energy building a career I wouldn't enjoy. I couldn't afford not to give this new venture a try.

This, I believe, is at least part of the motivation of most people who successfully start a new business: a feeling that if they never tried they would always regret it. It is what gives you the momentum to get out the front door, to cut the corporate umbilical cord, and what makes it possible to keep going, even when everything else makes you feel like turning back. Starting a business is a financial and professional commitment. But even more, it is an emotional one.

I have a friend who, five years ago, started what has become a very successful apparel manufacturing firm. He told me recently that if he had known then what the first two years were going to be like he would have never gone through with it.

We never had it that rough, but I could relate to what he was saying. There are so many moments in starting a new business when the negatives outweigh the positives that any feelings of satisfaction are very small compensation. There are times when it is the emotional commitment alone that keeps you going.

Ask Hard Questions

Starting a new business is no time for self-deception, yet it is quite tempting to get caught up in your own notes, business plans, and prospectus, in the romance of your own words and numbers.

You should be able to "state your business" clearly and succinctly. Is it a "hard" idea (a new product or one that fills a clearly defined void) or a soft one (certain consulting businesses, an already crowded industry, or an idea that isn't all that indistinguishable)? The danger, at the beginning, is that everything is still fiction and that fiction can block your ability to ask the right questions and provide the necessary hard-core answers:

What Are the Connections?

How does the idea connect to the market, to the time, and ultimately to the people who will have to buy it? What edge does it have over existing competition?

I have seen many new consulting businesses go under because the idea wasn't very good in the first place. In fact, it amazes me how often people think someone will pay for their expertise when theirs is not an essential expertise to begin with and when they have no monumental personal success stories to convince potential customers otherwise.

If I were starting IMG today in the same way as I did twenty years ago, I'm not all that sure it would work, and

I'm almost certain it would not have worked to the degree that it has. Arnold Palmer was the right person to represent at a time when the sport of golf was growing by leaps and bounds. A decade later, with our representation of Laver, then Newcombe, and then Borg, we were able to repeat this success in tennis, and now, again ten years later, we are positioned to do the same thing in running, though no stratospheric superstar has yet emerged in this sport.

In the first two instances, however—golf and tennis— while there is a sizable core market, there has been a flattening out of the growth curve.

If I were forced to repeat IMG's initial success today, I would have to wait for the right combination of factors—the connections—to come along: an emerging new participant sport; one with seeming whirlwind growth potential; and a superstar who embodied the essence of that sport.

Why Won't It Work?

What are the immediate problems likely to be encountered? Are they insurmountable, and if they aren't, how do I go about solving them?

What Makes Me Think I'm the One to Make It Work?

The new businesses that are most likely to succeed are the ones that have some relation to what you are already doing for someone else. In my case, IMG was not so much a new business as an extension of what I was already doing for a law firm.

Several years ago a friend of mine started a very success- ful photo reproduction business, which he later began to franchise. One of his franchisees, whose background was in lithography and design, was in trouble. After meeting with him in an attempt to straighten out the problem, my friend told me, "Just because our product is twice the quality at half the cost of our competition, he didn't think he had to go out and *sell* it. When I pointed this out to him, he said, 'Oh, but I'm not a *salesman!*' "

The dream of opening a restaurant, a frequent new business fantasy and a project with one of the highest mortality rates, is an example of why businesses fail because of the wrong aptitudes of their founders.

Restauranteering is a margin business which demands shrewd buying and a head for numbers. One should also be naturally gregarious and have a fondness for people and a willingness to work incredibly long hours.

Yet I have known a number of people who talked about opening a restaurant because they wanted "to do something different" and their sole qualification was that they were good cooks or liked to eat.

What Is the "Doability" Quotient?

We were once presented with a proposal for a World Air Race to coincide with the 1984 Olympics. The initial investment was around $3 million, and it was already partially funded. The concept was quite detailed and well presented. The only problem was that its execution required the cooperation of half the air forces in the world and an equal number of permissions to use air space.

Needless to say, the "doability" of this project was absurdly low. A good idea requiring reasonable expenditures may still be wrong because it is next to impossible to do, or, even if it can be done, the time required to execute it is far too high. Projects like this can have you working for fifty cents an hour.

Start Small and Keep It Simple

Many new venturists are preoccupied with all the money they are going to make rather than how they are going to go about making it. Set realistic goals by setting realistic steps—discrete, "doable" actions, each of which connects to the next one in some logical progression.

At some point you have to walk through the wall to get to the other side. But don't just "do it" until you have a good idea of what you do next. If you can't get "there" from "here" in a number of very specific steps, then you probably don't have a business yet.

I am a great believer that the more up-front money a new business requires the less chance it has of ever getting off the ground.

I'm prejudiced, of course, having started my own business with capitalization of less than $500. I am also aware there is a whole industry of venture capitalists who do nothing but fund new businesses. But the mere existence of this industry has created a kind of entrepreneurial myth—that there are all these people standing in line waiting for the opportunity to give you money and that you just haven't met any of them yet.

If and when you do, you will probably find that they aren't as eager to part with their capital as you might have anticipated, or, if they are, they will want to extract a large piece of the business in return for their faith.

Many new businesses never get off the ground, not because they were bad ideas, not because the people were wrong, but because the fund-raising efforts failed. Yet many of these new ventures, I believe, didn't actually require the capital the participants convinced themselves that they did. If they had been willing to start small, to go back a few steps and start from further back, they could have given themselves a fighting chance.

I can't overemphasize the importance of starting small and keeping it simple. When I began it would have been very easy to convince myself that it simply couldn't be done on any less than a million dollars. How could I represent the top three superstars in the booming sport of golf without a staff of seven or eight and at least a token presence in England and Japan? A million dollars, in fact, would have been helpful and certainly convenient. But it wasn't necessary.

Many of the great American success stories emerged from humble beginnings. If you are selling a service, a skill, or an expertise, how much more do you really need than a desk and a phone?

Be Flexible

Just as it is essential to know what business you're really in, it is equally important to be aware of what new business you *might* be in—of new directions and other opportunities which present themselves in the course of your doing business.

If you are tuned in and appropriately flexible, you may find that your original business is the tail and the new business it suggests is the dog. I have an acquaintance whose business is lecturing to corporations on effective writing techniques. He discovered that many companies were so impressed with his course they were willing to pay whatever he asked to write their corporate brochures for them. This has become a far more lucrative business for him than lecturing.

As I have mentioned, new divisions in our company grew out of our flexibility—the most obvious example being our marketing consulting division. We discovered in selling the services of our clients to various corporations that often our ideas as to how those clients should be used (how to position a particular athlete, what kind of campaign to structure, and so forth) were as valuable as the individual services themselves.

Share Your Success

In any business, new or otherwise, the idea is to take in more than you spend, but this is most painfully obvious when running a small, new operation.

Pay the people working for you as little as possible and sell them on yourself, on your vision, and on their future and the promise that as the company grows and becomes successful they will make more than they could ever make elsewhere. I don't think there is anything whatsoever wrong with this as long as you keep your end of the bargain.

If someone working for you makes a substantial contribution to the company, he or she is entitled to considerably more than the satisfaction of a job well done. In business, one's income acts as a scorecard. And while the company's overall profitability must be taken into consideration, that is going to matter a lot less to that executive than it does to you. Whether such tangible financial proof comes in the form of a raise, a bonus, or additional perks, it is important that people feel they are participating directly and commensurately with their contributions to the company.

Double Your Overhead

Several years ago I asked a friend who was starting a new business what he anticipated his overhead would be for the first year. He was starting small and financing it himself, and he replied in the neighborhood of $75,000. I told him at the time that he would be advised to double that amount.

People fail to take into account all the hidden costs in starting a new operation. It probably stems from a subconscious overzealousness to make the numbers work (or at least make them palatable). In any case, it's easy to forget about withholding and social security taxes when you've become accustomed to having them automatically deducted from your paycheck. Pens and pencils don't cost much, but supplying an office—even a small one—for a year adds up. Most businesses require some travel and entertainment, and that gets expensive. Utilities are extremely easy to underestimate. Last year our phone bill alone was over a million dollars. Over the years I've discovered that if you double the hard operating expenses you originally budgeted you'll end up with a reasonably accurate projection figure.

Recently I ran into the friend to whom I had given the advice. He told me that at the time, since I knew very little about his initial operation—what his rent and personnel were going to cost, and so on—he felt that it had been a fairly arrogant thing for me to say. "But when I closed the books at the end of the first year," he said, "the total was almost exactly $149,000."

Double It but Don't Triple It

Many people who want to start a new business but can never seem to get out the front door have convinced themselves that it is just a matter of waiting until they have enough money saved up. For these people $10 million would be just short of what they need.

No amount of money in the bank is going to compensate for the loss of security that accompanies the loss of a paycheck.

In working out your business plan, if you find yourself allowing for the maximum conceivable amount in every expenditure column, your plan will probably never be more than a mental exercise.

Income First/Organization Later

Good organization is essential to any successful operation. But there is something nonsensical about a brand-new corporation sporting an impressive five-year plan before it has even earned its first dollar. It's one thing to know where you're headed (or where you'd like to be headed). It's another thing entirely to practice "cart before the horse" planning.

Prospectuses Versus Real Life

I would be quite happy if I never saw another prospectus. The only ones who end up believing them are the people who write them.

The vast majority of the prospectuses I have been shown or invited to finance reveal a warped time perspective. It's amazing how many people forget to consider the importance of cash flow in planning their first year. If the first sale is made during the first week of business, very often the proceeds from the sale won't be collected for ninety days, and so on for the second and third sale, the result being, of course, that the initial float required for the business is actually a multiple of what's been projected on paper.

It is also amazing how blatantly obvious people are in padding their numbers. Allowing for a reasonable margin of error in the numbers is one thing; assuming stupidity on the part of the person reading them is another. I've seen proposals for business ideas which I thought had merit but which have so turned me off by the projected income and expense numbers that I lost faith in the people doing the proposing. I suspect that these people don't believe in the business themselves and are merely trying to con someone into financing a big expense account.

I have also seen prospectuses in which I knew the principal had factored in a salary for himself that was more than he was presently making as an employee. I don't think asking someone to finance a $2 million proposal is a very effective or efficient way to go about getting a $50,000 raise. I know for sure I don't want to be the one giving it to him.

Motion Versus Accomplishment

Being self-employed is the purest form of capitalism and the best way I know of getting paid what you are truly worth. It also demands a different mind-set, including an awareness that the number of hours you put in is only meaningful in terms of what you do with them.

Most successful entrepreneurs spend twenty-four hours a day either working or thinking about their business. But it is how they fill those hours that makes the difference between success and failure. The cliché is, "Don't work hard, work smart." The truth is, "Work hard, work long, *and* work smart."

On the positive side, in the beginning, when you are not having to deal with meetings and memos and all the other internal corporate time-takers, you can add, literally, four or five hours to every day. But if you don't spend them productively, not only will the difference be "deducted from your pay"; you might as well spend them writing memos to yourself.

Don't Have Partners

Not enough people examine their motives for taking on partners as carefully as they should. Often it is a safety-in-numbers factor. Naturally it is comforting to know that the buck doesn't necessarily stop at your desk. However, the problems of any partnership are likely to be a lot greater than the degree of security partnership is presumed to provide.

Obviously there are situations in which the strengths and weaknesses of each partner are well balanced and the business benefits from them. But the odds are a lot greater that the partnership itself will become the business's worst enemy, if only by limiting its flexibility. It is probably not an accident that some of the greatest entrepreneurial successes have been solo acts.

Don't Take Equity

Minority equity in a privately held corporation is, for my money, worthless. Having a "piece" of someone else's new venture is merely a twenty-four-hour ego trip, but I've always wanted to know exactly what it is they think they have. With minority equity in a sole proprietorship you cannot read the *Wall Street Journal* and see what you're worth; you cannot go to the bank and pledge the equity against a loan for a new home. You can't even sell the equity easily because such a sale will be restricted by the major shareholder, or else you'll find that no one will pay anything remotely resembling what *you* perceive the equity to be worth.

On many occasions we have taken advantage of misconceptions about minority equity. When our clients are offered equity in a new venture, I always insist upon fees in addition to equity or at least a guaranteed buy-back position at any time at the option of our client.

Fear of Failure

Fear of failure is at least as common as the desire for success. In fact, if properly harnessed it can be the energy that drives the wheel. But for many people it becomes debilitating.

Learning to use fear rather than letting it use you is obviously not just a problem for entrepreneurs but for anyone in business. Therefore it seems an appropriate point on which to end the book.

The French Olympic hurdler, Guy Drut, found himself in an unenviable position in the early summer of 1976. He was France's only hope for a track-and-field medal, and the burden of carrying the nation's pride on his shoulders was getting to him. Drut later told me that he had spoken on several occasions prior to the games with our long-time client Jean-Claude Killy and that he really felt he owed a part of his gold medal to Killy. He explained it as follows: "Jean-Claude told me that I was the only one who knew how to get my body and mind to their ultimate peak for the Olympic Games. He then told me that after I had done this that I should keep saying to myself, 'I have done everything I can to get ready for this race and if I win, everything will be great, but if I don't win my friends will still be my friends, my enemies will still be my enemies, and the world will still be the same.' I repeated this sentence to myself before the qualifying heats and during the break between the semi-finals and finals. I kept saying the sentence over and over, and it blocked out everything else. I was still repeating it to myself when I went up to get my gold medal."

Epilogue:
The
Inner Game
of Business

WHEN I COMPLETED the writing of this book, I gave the manuscript to a number of business associates. The response of some of them left me with one nagging concern.

Several of them told me, only half in jest, that they enjoyed the book "because I am already doing most of what you recommend." While this was meant to be flattering, I think they were glossing over those sections where their own business practices could stand the most improvement.

The worst thing this book could do is to engender any sort of self-satisfaction or complacency in those who read it. These are the most sinister forces in business and, alone, are powerful enough to inhibit advancement or career success.

Business is a competition, and any high-level, sophisticated competition is almost exclusively a head game. The Inner Game of Business, as this could be called, is understanding the Business Paradox: the better you think you are doing, the greater should be your cause for concern; the more self-satisfied you are with your accomplishments, your past achievements, your "right moves," the less you should be.

I have long been fascinated, both professionally and psychologically, by what makes a champion. By this I mean the true champions, the legends, the upper one percentile who consistently dominate their opponents, perform at their highest level at the most crucial times, and, in the long term, distance themselves from the near-greats and the also-rans.

Certainly skills and a supreme confidence in these skills are a part of it, but they are not the determining factors. Most athletes, by the time they reach the professional level, are already blessed with an abundance of both.

The champion's true edge exists solely in the mind, and over the years I have observed three attitudinal characteristics which are common to every superstar I have ever known. They are just as applicable in business as they are in the athletic arena. I have, in fact, adapted them to my own business career and they are the source from which I derive most of my drive and determination.

The first is the champions' profound sense of dissatisfaction with their own accomplishments. They use any success, any victory, as a spur to greater ambition. Any goal that is attained immediately becomes the next step toward a greater more "unreachable" one.

The second is an ability to peak their performances, to get themselves up for major tournaments and events. No one can operate consistently at his or her highest level, yet the legends of any sports era always seem to perform at their best when the stakes are the greatest. This is particularly true in tennis and golf, perhaps the most mentally demanding of all the major sports, and why the major tournaments in both have always been dominated by a handful of players.

Finally it is their ability to put their opponents away. This is referred to as "the killer instinct," but that tells you more about the result than of what is going on mentally.

In the champion's mind he is never ahead. He distorts reality to serve his competitive purpose. He is always coming from behind, even when the score indicates he is destroying his opponent. He never believes he is performing as well as he actually is.

I became acutely aware of this a number of years ago when I was in Osaka, Japan, watching Arnold Palmer and Gary Player play an exhibition match. As they made the turn, I ventured out from the clubhouse to join them on the ninth green. Arnold was lining up a ten foot putt for a birdie, and Gary, who had finished the hole, had walked over and was standing next to me with his arms folded. Though it was only an exhibition, these two champions were going head-to-head, and I could feel their intensity.

Arnold sank his putt, and Gary, shaking his head, turned to me and said, "He's been doing that all day. I can't buy a putt, and once he gets it on the green it's in the hole."

I found this remark a bit curious, because in reality, Arnold's birdie had brought them dead even.

As Arnold walked toward me on his way to the tenth tee, I could see he too was upset. "Well what do you know," he said, "I finally made a putt." Then, motioning ahead to Gary, he added "...and *that* little son-of-a-bitch has not missed one."

So, if this book has left you feeling satisfied with your own business acumen...you may have a lot of catching up to do.